big love

for the Thrive Factor Framework™ and her 12 Archetypes

"Meeting my Thrive Factor Archetypes with Shannon in 2018 was such an insightful experience. Learning about my core Archetypes has given me a new level of understanding and acceptance and truly given me permission to be me. I love this profiling and coaching so much that I jumped at the chance to become a Licensed Certified Thrive Factor Coach so I can help other women embrace themselves and give themselves permission to shine"

 Kim Herman

"What an incredible tool this is that Shannon has created. It has helped me completely understand what supports me in business and also what holds me back. I can't recommend a Thrive Factor Experience, meeting your Archetypes and working with Shannon enough!"

 Sam MacDonald

"I absolutely loved everything about my Thrive Factor Experience with Shannon. Discovering my four major Archetypes has given me such a deeper understanding of myself both personally and in business. Learning about myself in this way has given me invaluable tools in how I operate. I highly recommend Shannon's book The Thrive Factor also! I refer to it most days and it's become a guide for life and business now that I am also a Thrive Factor Coach"

 Kerryn Slater

"I'm so grateful to Shannon for creating Thrive Factor. I learned so much about myself and why I do what I do. I am totally an Inspirer Believer and I now embrace that girl 100%. Thank you gorgeous Shannon"

 Natalie Briney

"Thank you Shannon. My Thrive Factor Experience session was surprising and enlightening. Some Archetypes I recognised easily, and others were OH WOW! The real juiciness of finding out my Archetypes was how they flow and work together, and this is what has helped me use the archetypal energy for greatest benefit and results in my work. Knowing the strengths and potential challenges each one represents and how they can support and balance one another. After having the session, I was so thrilled that you wrote a book and it is such a beautiful handy reference to have. Plus, I love the fun images that you painted for the Archetypes"

 Aesha Kennedy

"Understanding my thrive factor Archetypes (Liberator Engineer here!) helped me see why I needed to let go of complicated systems and embrace simplicity in my marketing. I was also able to leverage my other archetype, Queen Ruler which I was resisting because of its negative stereotype. Once I could see how I could lean into my inner Queen, I was able to step up as a better leader without turning my followers into a clique. I am so glad that I did this with you Shannon and got a better insight into what makes me, me!"

 Swapna Thomas

"Being profiled by Shannon and discovering my Thrive Factor Archetypes, was a wonderful moment. Knowing about my Archetypes has given me so much more clarity and confidence in accepting and believing in myself and my strengths, whilst balancing my challenges. Thank you, Shannon, it really has helped me to be more in my 'effortless success zone'. I am so excited about becoming a Thrive Factor Coach!"

 Rachel Gardiner

"Looking at what I want to accomplish in my business through the lens of my Thrive Factor profile has made decision making easier for me. It's helped me to understand how to speak to my community, of course, but it's also helped me feel even more confident that I'm moving in the right direction. On top of all that, I've used it to help understand who I'm working with and clients. A valuable tool that I highly recommend!"

 Stasha Washburn

"I had the opportunity to have meet my Thrive Factor Archetypes with Shannon at a Symposium in Tuscany in 2018. I thought I had it all sussed out, I knew which Archetypes I was going to be. Boy did I get it wrong!! Shannon blew my mind! There was a moment of…"no no, you have that wrong", but that quickly unravelled with Shannon's incredible knowledge, experience and what this profiling and coaching is actually all about. In that single session, the beginning of my Thrive Factor experience, Shannon changed the way I see myself, not just as a businesswoman, but as a woman. I felt like I had full permission to actually be me and do things my way. And that was ok, it would still be successful. I cannot recommend this work enough, it truly is a game-changer"

 Amy Towle

"I had my Thrive Factor profiling completed by Shannon in 2019. And wow, what an insight! By understanding and knowing my Archetypes, I am now able to effectively use my strengths personally and professionally. I also now know what signs to look for when my body needs a rest and what also inspires me. Thanks Shannon. This is so valuable"

 Sarah Chopra

"After having my Thrive Factor Experience with Shannon it seemed to connect all the boxes. It was a significant aha moment. It gave me permission to just be me and explained a lot of the things that I knew but couldn't equate into daily life and business. I can't recommend it more highly, when you embrace your Archetypes you can leverage your strengths effortlessly. It also helps you recognise your challenges and understand what to do when they go from being potential to being real. Just do it!"

 Donna Gordin

"Shannon's Thrive Factor Experience and book have proven themselves real eye openers in my life. When I feel like I'm hitting a wall, in any facet of my life, I now know the strengths and potential challenges within me that I need to utilise and satisfy, to live a life that is more successful and effortless. An amazing framework that I recommend every woman familiarise herself with. Thank you, Shannon, for introducing me to me!"

 Stephanie Powell

BRAGAUDACIOUS
the art of BOLD self celebration

A year long guided experience for women inspired & determined to totally thrive & have loads of fun at the same time!

BY SHANNON DUNN

Visionary Creator of the Thrive Factor Framework™
Author of the international award winning
The Thrive Factor: Unlock your effortless success zone

Foreword by Cassie Howard

Disclaimer Please Read

Copyright© 2022 Shannon Dunn | All Rights Reserved.

The people, events and stories depicted in this book are for educational purposes only. They offer a representation of only some of what is possible for an individual. All names and details published are believed to be correct at time of printing. Whilst every attempt has been made to verify information provided in this book, the author accepts no responsibility for any errors, inaccuracies or omissions. The examples within this book are not intended to represent or guarantee that everyone or anyone will achieve their desired results. The success of each individual will be determined by his or her personal desire, dedication, effort and motivation. There are no guarantees you will achieve your desired outcome. The tools, stories and information are provided as examples only and not as a guarantee you will experience the same or even similar results.

First edition 2022 | Copyright 2022 Shannon Dunn

All rights reserved. No part of this book may be reproduced, stored in a retrieval system or transmitted in any form - electronically, mechanically, as a photocopy, via recorded means or otherwise without prior written permission of the author and publisher Shannon Dunn.

OTHER BOOKS BY SHANNON DUNN

The Thrive Factor: Unlock Your Effortless Success Zone (2019)
Personal Leadership Style: How to lead your life with effortless confidence, happiness and purpose (2013, no longer in print)
The Power of 100 [contributing author]
Ready, Aim, Influence [contributing author]
Sell Your Story [contributing author]

RELATED PROGRAMS, PRODUCTS AND SERVICES

To work with or learn from Shannon or a connect with a Certified Thrive Factor Coach™ (Licensed)
Visit **www.theThriveFactor.com**

To train with Shannon to become a Certified Thrive Factor Coach™ visit **www.thethrivefactor.com/certification**

To engage Shannon for business and leadership coaching and enrol in her business education programs, each infused with the Thrive Factor Framework™ visit **www.thrivefactorco.com**

All current opportunities to learn from, work with and connect with Shannon and Team Thrive Factor can be found at **www.thrivefactorco.com/shannon-dunn-links**

PUBLISHER

Self Published
ISBN: 978-0-9875892-3-1 (paperback)
ISBN: 978-0-9875892-5-5 (ebook)

Creative Possibility Outcomes PTY LTD trading as Thrive Factor Co
P.O. Box 240 Scarborough, Western Australia, Australia 6922
hello@thrivefactorco.com
www.thrivefactorco.com

CONTRIBUTORS

Author: Shannon Dunn
Foreword: Cassie Howard
Archetype Images: All Images of the 12 archetypes are the original artwork of Shannon Dunn and protected by copyright ©
Back cover photography images of Shannon: Selfies taken by the author.

foreword

I'm a born entrepreneur. I've been building businesses since I was a young girl having yard sales in her backyard every day in the summer. For the past 18 years, I've been building businesses online, and during this time, I've seen a lot, and heard a lot, about what it takes to build a successful business.

What propelled me further and faster than anything I've ever discovered is celebration. Celebration of the milestones. Celebration of growth. Celebration of the impact. I noticed that the more I celebrated, the more my business grew and the more money I would make - not to mention how much happier and grateful these celebrations made me feel!

When I met Shannon, I learned really quickly just how important celebration was in her life. She's someone who celebrates everything. There's nothing too small to celebrate! This is one of my favourite things about her, and it's what made us such a good fit in working together this past year. I could tell that this was a woman who would stop at nothing to succeed, and that she would do it in a way where celebration was a big part of her process and experience. The relationship that I have had with Shannon takes my breath away. Over the time I have known her, I have consistently been absolutely in awe of her. The power that this woman holds is so strong. The work she's doing in the world is massive. The impact she is having is incredible.

Shannon is one of the most loving, kind, yet fiercely badass women I've ever had the privilege of knowing. She's the founder of the Thrive Factor Framework™, which is similar to Human Design (but in my opinion, a lot easier to understand!), and once I learned about what this actually was and how it worked, I was hooked. I read all of her content online about it. I watched her lives on social media. I listened to her teach. And I haven't been the same since! I have had the ability to witness Shannon in her magic every single day, in a way not many others do. It is such an incredible privilege! I want to share her with you, because I believe you will benefit tremendously from having her in your life.

A few months ago, Shannon kindly led me through a Thrive Factor Experience, where she explained what my Archetypes were and what they meant, in great detail. I learned so much about myself in that session, and I took the messages she shared with me to heart and started implementing them in my business right away. I found a new sense of even greater ease in my life. Once I learned of my Thrive Factor Archetypes (author note, Cassie has the most powerful combination of 5 Archetypes) and how they work together, I understood myself on a level so deep that my whole world changed. It's no surprise that I went from $100K to $200K months in my business soon after this session with Shannon and now I am at consistent $300K months.

I want the world to know her.
I want the world to know her work.
Follow her, learn from her, buy from her, hire her.

This woman is absolute magic, and your life will never be the same once you step into her world.

The power of celebration in our lives cannot be understated, and there's no one I know that's better at helping you to understand this power (and activate it within yourself) than Shannon. The way Shannon teaches the art of celebration is in line with the way she models and teaches thriving, through her creation, the Thrive Factor Framework™ and it's 12 Archetypes.

When Shannon asked me to write this foreword, I was speechless. "Who, me? Write a book foreword? Can I?" I doubted that this was something I was worthy of. Then, I remembered the power of celebration, and I celebrated the fact that I get to be a small part of something that I believe is going to change the world. This book. I'm humbled, I'm grateful, and I'm celebrating.

I hope you're ready for a life-changing experience... the experience of eternal celebration of yourself and everything else in your life as Shannon calls it, it's being Bragaudacious.

Cassie Howard
The Limitless Woman

December 2021

always grateful

Writing this piece is always a heartfelt experience. It is the last thing to be added to a manuscript, a creation that often takes months to years to write. Piecing together each considered contribution is not something to be rushed. Along the way people flow in and out of your life, your community, your world, and it can be challenging to remember everyone to say thank you to who has, in small and large parts, contributed to this creation.

I have some key people who have been a part of this from its infancy, a small idea in my expansive creative brain, influenced by the incredible, ingenious women I have the honour of working with as coach, teacher, mentor, and cheerleader each day in the context of my work delivered by my coaching and consulting company, Thrive Factor Co and through the Thrive Factor Coach™ certification offered via Thrive Factor School. You know who you are. So much love to you.

To every one of you who has engaged with me when I've asked, "and what are you celebrating today/this week/this month/right now?" Thank you for your patience and playing along, often indulging my request, sometimes with great discomfort as you open yourself to understanding the pivotal role of celebration and self celebration for you in every facet of your life and the work you do.

I know it's often not an easy thing to do. I appreciate how much you have stretched yourself. I am so over the moon excited when I sense the shifts in you. Often subtle at first and then the tide of self celebration gains momentum and you begin our conversations, our group sessions, our mentoring experiences, our retreats boldly and excitedly telling me what you're celebrating long before I have had a chance to ask. With the shift I see your confidence expand, your resilience evolves, your self awareness grows, your ability to meet all parts of yourself with compassion, wisdom, curiosity, kindness, grace, and love, become your new usual.

It is this that motivates me, because when all this happens you unlock your effortless success zone. You thrive. Others thrive because you thrive, and the world becomes a better place because it has you in it. Yes, to more of that for us all. A joy filled, thrive activation that ripples out into the time and space, impacting so many. How can we be anything but more of who we are collectively – ingenious, determined, rebellious, wise, kind, inspirational, freedom loving, creative women - when this is our actualised reality?

There are over 40 incredible women who answered my call for contributions sharing how they celebrate in life, work, business. Each of these women are important to me in one way or another. Many I have known a long time and others are newer connections. Being active online as a business woman has supported me to expand my network of individuals who inspire me daily by being who they are. Thank you to each and every one of you for your enthusiasm when I messaged you to ask you to share. Your words are valued and appreciated, as are you.

Abundant gratitude to Cassie Howard, my business mentor during the time I was also creating this book. Your love of celebration and enthusiasm and support for my creations made it so effortless to ask you to write the foreword. Thank you inspirational Queen for saying an excitable yes!

I also wish to say a huge thank you to my family. When I dive into a writing experience, I tend to throw myself all in. It is intense and there is not a lot of time for simply just catching up. By no way do I neglect those who are important to me – I don't know how to do that – but I am less available. My focus becomes concentrated, as it needs to be to bring something as significant as a deeply loved and nourished piece of work, like a book to life.

Thanks to my frequently cheerleading Mum for all the support and infinite and often overwhelming belief in all I say I intend to do. I know sometimes what I share can sound wildly unrealistic, but you listen and encourage me and remember to check in with whatever my current creative indulgence is. Our Archetypes don't always find harmony, but I am thankful for the interest you show in this work and for listening as I explain where my big ambition, intense creativity and need for freedom come from. How grateful I am for your support and for the support I feel from Dad, even though it is now a number of years since he left this earthly field. Thanks Mum. Love you!

Thanks to the youngsters in my life.

My nieces Ruby, Mia and Hollie and nephew Ritchie. I love how Ruby and Mia are energetic, nature loving, kind and caring teens and finally old enough for us to officially discover their Thrive Factor Archetypes in the years since The Thrive Factor book was published. It has been a true joy seeing you express your innate selves in the world, and I am so happy you only occasionally roll your eyes at me when I say, "well your Archetype…" and then listen to what I have to share. I am even happier when you ask for my insight into something in your life where we can talk through things from the lenses of your Archetypes. How interesting it will be in the future when we get to know what Hollie's Archetypes are! I'll happily take bets on what they'll be from anyone who knows our energiser bunny of a spirited 5 year old soul who lights up any space she enters with her big, bold, loud personality.

Thanks to their awesome parents, my brothers, and sisters-in-law. I so appreciate you allowing and supporting me to be the kind of Auntie I am.

It would be remiss of me to forget to say thanks to my furball sidekick Archie cat. He shows up to crash Zoom sessions, to take up most of the screen when I go live on social media, to join your calls, to be present in a big way. I've always adored animals and having pets has been a constant in my life, but I can't say I've ever had a companion like this dude. I love how my clients ask where he is when he doesn't join me online. He's demanding, smothering, always knows when I need some company. His King Ruler, Hero Adventurer energy is palpable and adored. Thanks for being in my world buddy.

Big love to one and all for any impact you have had on the creation of this book. I am so excited to bring it to life and share it with the world. Your support, in all the ways it has been shared, means everything.

Celebrating you.

One and all!

contents

Foreword	VIII
Always Grateful	X
Introduction	1
The Importance of Self Celebration	1
Your Bragaudacious Year	6
Thoughts on Resistance to Celebration	7
Celebrate in Your Own Way	10
8 Tips for the Boldest Experience of Self Celebration in Your Bragaudacious Year	14
The Thrive Factor Archetypes	15
The Thrive Factor Archetypes and Strengths	18
The Thrive Factor Archetypes and Potential Challenges	19
The Gift of Afformations	21
Advocate Rescuer	24
Heroine Adventurer	36
Inspirer Believer	52
Liberator Engineer	68
Mediator Diplomat	83
Mentor Teacher	98
Mother Nurturer	115

Networker Connector	**131**
Pioneer Seeker	**147**
Queen Ruler	**162**
Shapeshifter Alchemist	**178**
Visionary Creator	**193**
Bragaudacious Sister, this is just the Beginning!	**211**
The Thrive Factor Coaches and Celebration	**214**
Meet Shannon	**217**
Become a Thrive Factor Coach™	**220**

introduction

The Importance of Self Celebration

There is not enough self celebration being expressed by women in the world. Now that is out in the open, I want to say I'm determined to change that. So determined that I've given the art of bold self celebration a name and turned it into its own thing. A living expression of celebration in the world. To celebrate boldly, creatively, fully, wildly, compassionately, inclusively, artfully is to be Bragaudacious.

Welcome to a year of self celebration. Your year of self celebration. Your year of being Bragaudacious. An experience that will, if you engage with it fully and regularly, change your life for the better.

A question I have often been perplexed by is "why is it that celebration of any kind is so difficult for a multitude of women the world over?"

"Why are some women so effortless with their celebrations, confidently declaring their latest accomplishments to the world, hot on the heels of a recent win, while others struggle to acknowledge even the smallest of things?"

I have pondered these questions often. Sometimes I feel I have insights and possible answers. Other times I've no idea what's going on. Seemingly no clue as to why this is something that's such a struggle for so many.

I'm not suggesting there's no celebration.

No.
There is celebration. At times.
It's frequently conditional celebration though.

Conditional on some imagined guidelines or expectations. Conditional on the stars and planets aligning a certain way. Conditional on someone else's encouragement perhaps. Conditional on external validation. Conditional on your curated life to share on social media being good enough when you compared to your peers. Maybe conditional as a form of security, safety even.

Conditional on too many things.

These conditions are robbing you of living life more fully. They're robbing you of experiencing a state you deserve to know - your state of totally thriving.

The conditions hold you back.
They limit you.
The conditions get in the way.
They can and will prevent you from things like positive emotions, being able to trust yourself and others, tapping into your wisdom, building confidence, making decisions, being more you each day.

In my work as a Coach working with women in leadership and business for close to two decades and backed by my experience as a Counsellor and Transpersonal Art Therapist, I've sat across a table, in circles, in rows in rooms with women from all walks of life. I've sat at my laptop and phone interacting with you online. I've stood at lecterns and on stages speaking and teaching you. In these times I have witnessed too many women

Apologise for existing.
Ignore their strengths.
Deny their accomplishments.
Deflect compliments.
Shy away from attention.
Defer to the next person who they believe to be more qualified, or deserving, or some other justification story made up in their head.
Diminish themselves.
Judge when others celebrate.
Judge when others draw any attention to them and what they have achieved.
Choose others over themselves.

Block their ambition.
Actively prevent themselves from celebration.

If you recognise your own responses to celebration opportunities in the list above that's awesome. You can change what you don't recognise. Now you have awareness, the first step to making a permanent shift in a new direction. One inclusive of self celebration.

I can put my hand up to own having experienced many of the things listed above.

I still have ingrained social, gender and cultural conditioning influencing my innate response to celebration despite making a conscious choice to actively celebrate me – who I am, who I am becoming, what I create and what I teach.

I still fall into a lifelong habit of celebrating others before I celebrate myself. It's a natural instinct for me to consider others first. I think the same may be the case for you. It is for women everywhere, irrelevant of who you are, where you are, what you do. It is also a trait of the Inspirer Believer Archetype that I, and many members of my fabulous community have.

That's ok. It is a fact.

But let's agree from this point forward that this is the start of a new way to be.
A new way to think.
A new way to act.
A new way to respond.
A new way to express and honour yourself in the world.

From this point forward the next year is an experiment in celebration. An experiment in celebrating you! An experiment in something I'm calling Bragaudacious; the art of bold self celebration with YOU as the star!

As you engage with this book and let her become part of your life, you'll discover all multitude of things come into existence when self celebration is what you do and who are a woman who knows how to celebrate. A woman who actually does celebrate, starting with herself first.

Consider this year as your chance to begin something that supports you for the remainder of your, hopefully, long and thriving life. See it as cultivating a practice. A practice that is one offering

Awareness
Consciousness
Intentionally
Permission
Possibility
Potentiality
Expansion
Freedom
Intuition
Wisdom
Humility
Creativity
Curiosity
Happiness
Comparison
Competition
Choice
Personal leadership

And cultivate this practice, your Bragaudacious year of self celebration, through the lenses of

Curiousity, where you explore with an inquisitive sense of intrigue. And you do so without attachment, judgment or making meaning of your discoveries.

Compassion, where you welcome your heart into the experience and approach everything with gentleness, kindness, self love and appreciation.

Ingeniousness, where you own the fact you have wisdom, a combined lived and learned experience and the reality it is all of incredible value as the embodiment of you expressed wisely in the world. Effortlessness, where you choose a path that is spacious, make decisions fuelled by belief it can be easier and by simply approaching everything with a "how can this be easier?" curiousness each time it feels challenging, overwhelming, heavy or hard.

Big love to you, ingenious superstar. Welcome to the self celebration infused Bragaudacious sisterhood!

your bragaudacious year

This book has been written for you to be a companion, a guide, a support, a friend. She's here to journey with you as you dive into a whole year of self celebration; your BRAGAUDACIOUS year.

Over the course of 12 months, you will explore what it means to celebrate all you are, all you've come from, all you've learned, all you are learning. You will celebrate the parts of you that you adore and the parts of you you'd rather, or used to, ignore.

You can start your Bragaudacious year at any point in the year. In fact, choose any month you like or feel drawn to and start there. This is your experience. You are in the driver's seat for the whole year, so uniquely make it your own. If you're on social media, share your celebrations with the hashtag #bragaudaciousmoment so I can find them and celebrate you!

Make it a year where you do what feels right and good and nourishing for you. A year where you let go of things that have interrupted or completely blocked your self celebration. A year where you see and honour the contribution you make and the impact you are creating. A year that is all yours. A year that will ripple out into the rest of your life as the gift that keeps on giving. A year where you understand and know what it means to celebrate and to thrive.

A year where your thriving means others thrive. This is something I love and call collective thriving. It is underpinned by my belief that it is every woman's birthright to know what it means to thrive and that the knowing is the start of experiencing it. I believe all people, the world over deserve to thrive, but my work and teachings are primarily for women and those identifying as female so I'll start there. And I know from my own lived experience and nearly five decades of exploring in the world, that when a woman chooses to know, understand, and celebrate herself she does activate and amplify her potential to thrive. In doing so she shows others what is possible, and the thriving expands into the world as others know what it means to thrive in their way.

So good.
So needed.

thoughts on resistance to celebration

I didn't originally plan to include this section but as I reached out to my global community and network of incredible women – women in business, entrepreneurs, leaders, dreamers, soul searchers, healers, guides, creatives, friends, mothers, sisters, grandmothers – I recognised an interesting pattern.

One I wanted to share for you, no matter your relationship with celebration and particularly self celebration. It is not always an easy thing to be open to and engage in celebration. There are realities playing out in your life and in the world that can compete with your desire or wish to celebrate at any level. While I am a demonstrative advocate for more celebration and self celebration I also know the realities of living through times when celebrating doesn't even enter my mind or my heart.

The writing of this book was a process of creating over about an 18-month period. It has coincided with a time in my life when I was emerging from the other side of a significant life shift; the end of my marriage in 2019 and subsequent divorce. The end of this arduous relationship that was not what I dreamed it would be was definitely something to celebrate, even though it didn't feel it in the immediacy of the end. The writing has also been at a time when I was in a space and place of realigning and coming home to myself. It was an opportunity to search my soul for my inner compass and reset the course for my future vision to become actualised. There were so many times when celebration and self celebration were way down on my list of priorities. Some days it was all about surviving and thriving was somewhere out there in the ether. Also, the more I showed up in my business with the energy of celebration, the more I could see and sense the expansion of things to celebrate across all areas of my life.

The writing phase of Bragaudacious was also a time when change in the world was rapid and unrelenting. A global pandemic is an interesting time to write about celebration. The duality of being human and of living with every possible emotion and experience playing out simultaneously internally and externally can be incredibly disconcerting. If you haven't been shaken up and shaken around somewhat since early 2020 than I don't know what kind of world you live in. I do know many who would be envious of your reality. But with the reality of what we have collectively lived through, celebration could feel like a distant experience you used to know, but no longer feel familiar with.

These realities and the ups and downs of life will continue to influence you in their unique ways for as long as you live. Sometimes the influences are large scale in terms of their impact and reach. At other times they are personal and very much focused on your immediate world and not the greater universe in which we all live. For now, let me get back to the observations I made when reaching out to my extensive and growing global community.

Initially I shared posts requesting thoughts, words, and contributions on how you celebrate in groups I am in on social media. Sometimes these requests received a few responses. There were other times that there was no response at all. I get the social channels can be super busy and it is easy to miss an important post or request from someone, even if you are actively following them. I wasn't despondent to the limited response to these requests. I am an optimistic realist at heart. I thank my Inspirer Believer Archetype for that trait. So I kept writing and reflecting and knew there would be another opportunity to share my request.

The real observation about celebration and our collective potential resistance to it came when I created a list of names of incredible women I have, at some time, probably in the time of writing this book, connected with in some profound way. Women who have inspired me. Women who have achieved so much growth. Women who are friends. Some I have known a long time. Some newer connections. I reached out with an invitation to send me a contribution as I had decided at the very beginning of mapping out the concept for the Bragaudacious book, that I wanted to include the voices of women worldwide sharing how they celebrate. I outlined what the book was about and shared context of how much to share as I had been asked multiple times for guidance on this. I explained who the book was for and why I wanted her to contribute. Then one of three things happened. And they happened in varying degrees. The third response was the one that got me in the feels though.

1. I got an excited and often rapid response with a "yes I want to contribute" and a "I'll send something ASAP" and then they followed through. Such beautiful words shared. Raw, real, vulnerable, excitable examples of celebration for themselves in life and work. No hesitation. Abundant gratitude for being asked. An enthusiastic willingness to be involved

2. The message and the one or two gentle nudges got ignored. That's completely fine. We get busy. I know what my messenger feed on Facebook and Instagram can be like. So busy at times that I can miss important messages or intend to go back and read them and they simply fall down the feed until I don't see them as unread messages. All good!

3. I got a response, but it was a decline. Often with a "I don't have anything to share" or "I don't have anything to celebrate" or "I don't celebrate" or "I'm not good enough to be in your book." These messages made me feel sad. I felt disappointed that so many women are in the world feeling like this. I felt disheartened that there are so many women – people – but women specifically in this instance – who felt they had nothing to share. I sensed judgement. I sensed fear. I sensed a whole range of not enoughness and I sensed sadness. I felt worthiness and deservability – a lack of both – present in their messages. I also became ignited and more determined than ever to get this book published and to open the conversation around celebrating in all its forms, with a compassionate emphasis on self celebration and an invitation for more of it.

There could be a range of reasons why celebration hasn't been a natural thing for you. There are some possible influences included in the next section.

I want to share with you that I wholeheartedly believe every individual on this planet is worthy of celebration. Just as I believe that every woman (and person) on this earth has a birthright to thrive. You deserve to experience celebration. You are as available to be in a state of celebration as much as the next person and the one on the other side of them. You are worthy. You are deserving. You living in the world each day is worth celebrating.

I want to end this topic by encouraging you to consider celebration and self celebration from a simple perspective. In the next section I share about celebrating your own way as an added encouragement to do what works for you. The very first step may be to open to the possibility of celebration. If it has not been something you've done often, or at all, then start with small steps. Baby steps even. An occasional celebration that works for you is still a celebration and so valuable. Celebration is not a volume thing – the quality of your celebration on your terms is far more important than the quantity and type of celebration.

I truly see, know, and trust that every individual globally has something to celebrate.

I see, know, and trust this like I believe there is always something to be grateful for.

Imagine if, celebration was something you simply did?
Imagine if, celebration was expansive and fun?
Imagine if, in celebrating others, you opened to the possibility of celebrating yourself more?
Imagine if, celebration was filled with gratitude, compassion, and love?
Imagine if, celebration was available all the time?
Imagine if, celebration was whatever I wanted it to be?
Imagine if, celebration was grounded and supported me to embody my experiences?
Imagine if, celebration…? (finish this any way you like!)

celebrate in your own way

I am a big believer in finding your own path. I believe in being YOU and releasing the often-pre-conditioned notion that fitting in means changing yourself to be like another, or others, to conform in some way, or many ways. I have learned in my nearly five decades on this earth that this is unnecessary and that adjusting yourself to fit in, with a desire to experience the same kind of success, happiness, love, and satisfaction as you see and know another woman is experiencing, is one of the greatest disservices you can do to and for yourself.

To conform is to give away or deny parts of you, to fall in line with another's ideas of what is acceptable. It is to change who you innately are. Sometimes I have observed conforming as a way to fit in. Sometimes it happens because you simply aren't yet sure or confident in who you are. I have seen it a lot in my multiple decades in business. At times it is easy to see what has contributed to the conforming, and at other times I am unsure as to why. I don't really need to understand why.

I want you to think about why you do what you do.
In life. In career. In business.
Are you intentionally making decisions, taking action, and finding your own way?
Learning to be ok with the unknown and the uncertainty?
Being uncomfortable while you shift into greater levels of comfort?
Opening to increased self awareness?

I believe finding your own path in the world and being YOU are foundational aspects of self awareness and important for a fully lived expression filled with self celebration.

I believe these things in relation to all aspects of life, career, and business. I believe these things in relation to celebration. In fact, trying to celebrate the way others celebrate, because you think it is how it's done, is not the way to celebrate. It could be completely out of alignment with who you are, what you believe, what you value. It probably won't feel like you think celebration will feel.

Celebration, like so many things in our lived experience, has diverse expressions. In today's world we often become witness to celebration via social media. We may also still get to partake in all kinds of celebrations with others for the milestones experienced. It could be for birthdays, life milestones, accomplishments, awards, through to just for the sake of it celebrations with family, friends, community. The extremes of celebration often influence the way you celebrate, or what you believe celebration to be, or why you believe celebration is warranted.

There are the brash, bold, loud, confetti, balloons, and bubbles (bubble machine or champagne!) kinds of celebrations you see plastered all over your social media channels and they may feel fun, enticing and enriching. It may be something you can't do just yet, but something you plan to do in the future. It may feel expansive and energising and leave you inspired and motivated. If it does, that is awesome! Celebrating you (and with you metaphorically) for all that!

But there is often a flipside. Seeing those kinds of celebrations on your social media feed may leave you with a feeling of dread, wondering how you're ever going to pull that kind of extravaganza off. Thinking it is the way people celebrate these days. It's just not your style, or it will cost more than the $$ you have available to spend right now. It feels frivolous, unnecessary and a waste of time and money. It seems like a lot of work and as though it is drawing attention to you and showing off from a place of ego. That is so not your jam. Side note: there are some Archetypes who are just not naturally wired to celebrate with ease and excitement! Nothing wrong with that. It's who you are.

The things influencing when and how you celebrate can be multifaceted. While this book has been written for all of you who are and identify as female, there can certainly be gender influences. There are also cultural influences. Some cultures are frequently loud and colourful, inclusive and lead celebrations with a more-the-merrier approach. Other cultures in the world are more private with their celebrations and less inclined to celebrate for no obvious, justifiable reason.

There are also generational influences. If I think about the age range of the women I have worked with as clients I have found many younger women find it easier to celebrate. That is not to say the older women in my community are less likely to celebrate, but often they have so many other things to juggle that celebration and focus on themselves is not a priority. Often, they have spent so much time caring for others that they have disconnected from the parts of themselves more inclined to celebrate. They don't consciously think to celebrate. Day's morph into each other, weeks pass by, years seem to vanish and somewhere in all that celebration got lost.

Another consideration to how open you are to celebration is related to mindset and beliefs. If you grew up in a family or environment where celebration was rare, then your comfort level celebrating may be different to the way your friend feels about and practices celebration based on her experience of celebration as a younger person. If celebration in the environment you spent the most time in as a child was looked down upon as and referred to as something other families did, then you may feel celebration to be a foreign experience and resist it, judge it, ignore opportunities to celebrate.

In contrast, if your family and those you spent time with growing up were big into celebration and acknowledging all kinds of things, then you will likely find celebrating others and yourself an easier thing to do. Your personal relationship with yourself is also an influencer on celebration. The messages I received that shared something along the lines of "I don't have anything to celebrate" immediately made me think about worthiness and deservability. I didn't send this quote from author Brene Brown, but I wanted to share it with so many people during the process of seeking contributions. If you need to read this, need to hear it, need to embody it, read silently, read out loud, feel into this quote as many times as you want to…

"when you get to a place where you understand that love and belonging, your worthiness, is a birthright and not something you have to earn, anything is possible."

If you were a woman who sent me a message saying you couldn't contribute, for any reason, or you didn't respond because you felt you had nothing to share, then know that I see you, I honour you, I believe in you, I celebrate you. And I believe, with every cell of my body and expression of my soul, that you can come to a place where you know what it means to celebrate and to celebrate yourself. My wish for you and all women reading this book is that you enjoy this guided journey to celebration and that, month by month, you build and nurture a nourishing relationship with celebration, on your terms, for you.

Also know that no way of celebrating is right or wrong. No one way of celebrating is better than another way. The most important aspect of celebrating is finding your own way to do it. It could be bold, loud and in your face. It could be quiet, private, and emotive. It could be shared with people important to you or shared on your social media channels. It may be solo and self-honouring in a unique, loving way.

As I love to say to the women I work with – the quiet rebel women of the world – ingenious, wise, ambitious, creative, soulful, compassionate beings – you are charting your own path, using your own compass, and engaging with the world on your terms. You always have a choice so act on that reality. While you're doing so, know that welcoming more celebration can make everything that much richer and rewarding.

How cool is that?

Cue the pom poms and a dash of confetti I say. Well my Inspirer Believer Archetype is in charge there, but I'm totally on board with her.

8 tips for the boldest experience of self celebration in your bragaudacious year

1. Buy yourself the most divine journal and pens to capture your learnings, insights, frustrations, and celebrations – capturing these regularly is you stepping into and opening to self awareness boldly and that is a beautiful thing indeed

2. Get a friend, or two or three or 10 or more and share the experience each month! Bragaudacious Club could totally be a thing. In fact, set one up and share on your socials with #bragaudaciousclub

3. Share in the online space and let the world know about your Bragaudacious moments by using the hashtag #bragaudacious or #bragaudaciousmoment when you post on social media

4. Set yourself monthly Bragaudacious goals and share them publicly so everyone you know can get on board – accountability through sharing with those who are important to you is incredibly motivating

5. Share your Bragaudacious moments regularly – we can't make this a revolution of self celebration if it is happening in isolation and super quietly. When sharing on social media add #bragaudaciousmoment so the growing sisterhood of women celebrating can find you!

6. Create your own Bragaudacious rituals to expand your celebrations (there's a creative exercise each month to help you with this)

7. Have fun, on the fabulous days, the challenging days and every day in between. Fun = expansion and expansion = the opportunity for more to celebrate AND more thriving individually and collectively!

8. Use the experience of your year of bold self celebration as a way to expand into more of who you are and to do so with conscious, considered, compassionate choice, joy, wisdom and curiosity.

the thrive factor archetypes

One of the things that makes this experience a totally unique one for many of you reading will be that it is also a year of self celebration infused with inspiration from the Thrive Factor Framework™ and her 12 Archetypes.

The Framework is the cornerstone of my purpose in this world and exists to connect women everywhere with her innate potential and birthright to know what it means to thrive. Founded on principles of archetypal psychology in 2010, the Framework and it's expanding teachings has become a much loved experience for women globally who are motivated to expand their self awareness and unlock their effortless success zone. Self celebration gets wrapped up in that experience at every step of your expression in the world of your Thrive Factor.

Think of meeting your Thrive Factor Archetypes as tapping into the psychology of you and doing so with the support of a proven, reliable body of theoretical and anecdotal research and observation stemming back to 2008 when the first idea to create a way for women to meet themselves with compassion, grace, wisdom and acceptance was born.

Each Thrive Factor Archetype has her own individual characteristics that are expressed in individual ways. These personal characteristics have been defined in relation to something referred to as the 4 M's of Momentum. They feature and are taught extensively in all my programs, private coaching, and group mastermind coaching experiences. The 4 M's of Momentum are mindset, marketing, money and magnetism.

If you have a copy of The Thrive Factor: Unlock your effortless success zone, my 2019 award winning book, or have followed me, been in my programs, or worked with a Certified Thrive Factor Coach™, the Archetypes will be familiar to you.

The origins of the word Archetype are founded in ancient language. Arche meaning first or original, and tupos meaning impression. An Archetype can be described as the first or original impression we have of someone. The word Archetype is more commonly used in everyday language than it was in the early days of my exploration into this space. It is, thankfully, more appropriately understood for what it actually means.

I attribute my interest in things that are not commonly understood or explored to my Visionary Creator Archetype. She is one of four I have in my Thrive Factor profile. I celebrate her for her futuristic intrigue and ability to tap into innovative, fresh ways to see, experience and understand. I also celebrate her gift of bringing the gifts and resources from future time and space to the present so the greater community can experience these for themselves.

Archetypal Psychology is a body of psychology focusing on the use of Archetypes and archetypal frameworks that offers deep connection to self awareness and self understanding for those seeking to live as whole, embodied versions of themselves. Archetypal Psychology principles underpin much of the Thrive Factor Framework™. Carl Jung is perhaps the most well known thought leader in the field of Archetypal Psychology and his foundational work with Archetypes, myth and story continue to shape the use of Archetypes in fields from psychology to business worldwide. You can find out more about him and some of the earlier, heavily psychology influenced Archetype frameworks and methodologies with a quick search online.

The Thrive Factor Framework™ was created for women exclusively, and those identifying as female. This is just one of it's unique attributes and an attribute greatly appreciated by the expanding community of Certified Thrive Factor Coaches (Licensed) and women globally who are living each day with the positive and nourishing influence of their Thrive Factor Archetypes.

As you learn more about the Thrive Factor Archetypes you will see reference to something we call your effortless success zone. Sounds like something you want to know about?

Your effortless success zone is the actualised state of increasing ease experienced when self awareness evolves from a learned to a lived, embodied experience. The more a woman actively uses her archetypal strengths and understands the impact of her potential challenges, she activates her potential expanded ease and thriving.

I'll share more about the strengths and potential challenges of the Thrive Factor Archetypes in the coming pages. If you want to meet your Thrive Factor Archetypes go to **www.thethrivefactor.com/bragaudacious** where you will find links to all the current resources and opportunities associated with the Bragaudacious book and meeting your Thrive Factor Archetypes.

You may have a combination of 3 to 5, even 6 of the possible 12 Thrive Factor Archetypes in your Thrive Factor Profile, but if you want to learn about one of them you can do that at **www.thethrivefactor.com/discover.** You will be able to take the complete Thrive Factor Assessment and meet one of your lead Archetypes. An amazing start to dip your toe into the world of thriving, in a Thrive Factor infused way.

The Thrive Factor Archetypes are

Advocate Rescuer
Heroine Adventurer
Inspirer Believer
Liberator Engineer
Mediator Diplomat
Mentor Teacher
Mother Nurturer
Networker Connector
Pioneer Seeker
Queen Ruler
Shapeshifter Alchemist and
Visionary Creator

Each Archetype has become the influence for a chapter in Bragaudacious, giving you a beautiful chance to get to know them all and to welcome their energy, their gifts, their strengths, their wisdom, their expression in you and in every woman. While you will have your own combination of Archetypes, I have always been a believer in one key teaching in traditional archetypal psychology, and that is a reality that we have aspects of all Archetypes within a framework present within us. I love recognising Archetypes in another woman and celebrating her for who she is and who she has the potential to become. It is such an exciting and very Inspirer Believer way to look at the world. Bring it on!

the thrive factor archetypes and strengths

In traditional archetypal psychology and its myriad of frameworks, methodology and expression globally you will find reference to the light and shadow of Archetypes. When I created the Thrive Factor Framework™ I created it for women, with a focus on women in business and leadership. With that intention I wanted to create language unique to the Framework and the business and leadership space. I chose to refer to the light of each Archetype as her strengths and to refer to the shadow of each Archetype as her potential challenges.

If we explore the light aspect through the lens of strength, know that each attribute, skill, mindset, appearance, manifestation, creation, trait, characteristic and so on for each Archetype is something 100% available to you. Even if you have no lived experience of it.

I have addictively loved hearing and seeing so many women I have personally worked with and introduced to her Thrive Factor Archetypes describe this discovery as permission giving and enriching. She has said things like "I like myself" and "I have so much of value I didn't realise I have" and "this is so exciting to see myself in this way" and even "I can celebrate this in so many ways!"

The Thrive Factor Coaches share the same kind of feedback and equally love hearing these kinds of things from their clients. How could you not have an overflow of feel-good vibes rippling out of you as you observe the subtle and equally powerful shifts and changes happening before your very eyes as you sit across from a client or meet her online to introduce her to her Thrive Factor Archetypes, or work with her, supporting her through the Thrive Factor coaching methodology to guide her to amplify her own thriving. Addictive in the best possible way.

Each of the 12 Thrive Factor Archetypes has an expanding number of strengths available to her.

As a valuable starting point, you can get to know them by investing in a copy of The Thrive Factor book. Published early 2019 it offers a thorough introduction to each Archetype, her strengths, her potential challenges and her personal way of conveying mindset, marketing, money and magnetism.

I am continuously gaining new insights, understandings and teachings about each Archetype and share these abundantly in my programs, my retreats, when speaking on stage and with my valued clients in every context I get to work with you. If you are an inquisitive soul who thrives on learning and immersion in both a lived and learned experience you are highly likely a Mentor Teacher, there is also a developing and increasing opportunity for you to learn more about yourself and the women in your world.

There are links in the previous section that point you where to find the most up to date ways to connect with all things Thrive Factor.

the thrive factor archetypes and potential challenges

The other side of your archetypal strengths are your potential challenges. When I first explored the shadow of each Archetype, I was able to quickly define challenges each could experience. Originally the shadow was referred to as challenges but over time and with expanded thinking and observation I came to understand that including the world potential with challenges was necessary. Not every challenge I document or share in my teaching is going to be experienced by a woman with that Archetype.

The reason is that each of your Archetypes influences your other Archetypes in different ways. So, you may have the same four Archetypes as I do and also have a fifth Archetype that completely changes the way the Archetypes we share show up for you. I love the individual and truly unique way the Archetypes coexist with each other and within you.

I want you to remember the word potential each time you consider one of your challenges and to know the power of that word in the context of things you may previously have considered aspects of yourself that were broken, wrong, things to be judged, criticised, parts of you that needed changing or fixing or eradicating completely.

There is nothing about you that is lacking value.
You are whole.
You are an incredible being who has so much to offer.
You matter.
Your impact matters.
You thriving is important and needed.

Read that again!

In fact, personalise it by changing each line to an "I statement" and turn it into a meme, or write it on a post it note or add it to your journal and read it daily.

Share it on your socials and be sure to tag #bragaudacious and #thethrivefactor when you do so myself and team Thrive Factor can share it too and in celebration you when we do. This is probably a good time to say that if you are an Instagram lover and create stories, that if you search stickers with the term thrivefactor you'll find a set of Thrive Factor inspired stickers and there is even a Bragaudacious one for you to use. So fun.

Before I move on, I want to say a little more about my decision to exchange the word shadow for the phrase potential challenges. Shadow as a word in a psychological sense often gets a bad rap. Unfairly so. I am not a fan of people calling themselves shadow hunters and going on a personal mission to hunt down the shadow aspects of themselves. I have found this is often done with an intention of eradicating them instead of integrating them.

Carl Jung defined shadow as those aspects of the personality that we choose to reject and repress. For one reason or another, we all have parts of ourselves we don't like, struggle with, or that we think society won't like. Our solution to dealing with them is often seen as to push those parts down into our unconscious psyches. This is what Jung referred to as our shadow self. We all have one. No one escapes having a shadow. In my experience, the greater your light in the world, or in Thrive Factor terms, the bolder your strengths, the larger the impact of your shadow could be. When I am teaching this in the context of business I often describe standing in full visibility as a bright light and remind my amazing and ingenious clients that the brighter they shine and the larger the light they are, the greater the size of the shadow they potentially cast in the world.

Shadow is not a bad thing. When I explored shadow in the context of my Transpersonal Art Therapy qualification, I came to understand that it is the integration of the shadow aspects of yourself – acknowledgement and understanding of the treasure available within your potential challenges – that offers the greatest gift for any individual.

I frequently say that self awareness and self celebration are two of the most underrated opportunities for any woman (or man) who desires to live a fully expressed life, no matter what that life entails.

To live a fully expressed, thriving life, requires you to meet and know all parts of yourself. Meeting your shadow aspects, your potential challenges, and seeing them with eyes wide open for the wisdom they have for you is not something to fear. It is something to embrace. If you wish to do so with help, then please reach out to team Thrive Factor and we'll do what we can to connect you with the most appropriate support available at the time.

As mentioned previously, there are links in the previous section that point you where to find the most up to date ways to connect with all things Thrive Factor.

the gift of afformations

I love starting and ending my days with afformations. Unlike an affirmation which doesn't always work for me, my afformations are playful and give my creative brain lots of freedom to explore and dream of new realities. If affirmations have always left you wondering why people think they are so fab, then afformations may be about to become your new favourite go-to mindset reset tool. I have included them all the way through this book.

Sure, affirmations work for some people, but if your brain is wired a certain way they may just leave you with a "yeah, so what!" kinda feeling. Or you may find yourself thinking or saying "whatever" or laughing wildly at the statement you just said out loud that is so far from your truth and lived reality the only way to respond to it is hilarity.

If you have felt that success is out of your reach, saying "I am successful in every moment" can feel like a lie. If you have had experiences with money where your reality has been juggling funds week to week or month to month at a time then saying "I am a divine magnet for money" can feel like a mistruth at soul level.

If that is the kind of response you have to the 'fake it till you make it' energy that often sits behind affirmation teachings then turning affirmations on their head and tapping into the gift of how your brain is designed to work could be the revelation you have been seeking.

I have loved including afformation practices in so many of my programs, masterminds and Thrive Factor experiences the past couple of years and it is such a joy to see so many women relieved to have discovered something they are excited to try. No more "affirmations are useless." Instead, I hear "oh this is cool! I can't wait to try afformations." Totally time for a happy dance.

Afformations are the work of Noah St John. I don't remember when I first learned of them but it was one of those "where have these been all my life" kind of moments. They instantly made sense to me and were so useful that I use them daily, in all kinds of situations. Aside from the fact they made sense – which is also a great motivation to inspire action – I loved the fact that they work in harmony with the way the brain works. From my understanding and Mentor Teacher nerding out on afformations, I discovered that they were created as a framework to draw on the simplicity of neuroscience.

I also see that they work with the influence of our environment and reality that we live in a world focused so often on logic, proof and evidence. You don't need to feed logic, have proof or seek evidence to benefit from afformations. They don't play in that space. They love the landscape of imagination, dreaming, creativity, expansion, possibility and potentiality and seeking answers to questions. Parts of our thinking and emotional selves that are often overlooked.

Afformations are created as questions and most of us, according to neuroscience research, have brains that are wired to seek answers to the questions we ask.

I create all of my afformations with the phrases "imagine if" or "what if..." and then use the same kind of statement I would have used in an affirmation.

It isn't complex to create your own. Use the ones I have created for you each month and have fun with them. Their playful nature is good for your brain and your spirit and your future could change significantly just with challenging your thinking and engaging with fresh views, afformation style.

You will be able to access a free mini course on Afformations
at ***www.thethrivefactor.com/bragaudacious***

Month One
ADVOCATE RESCUER

archetype themes

Compassion, Boundaries, Harmony, Helping, Generosity, Kindness, Giving, Caring

goddess inspiration

Kwan Yin

This month we take inspiration from the Advocate Rescuer, the first alphabetically of the 12 Thrive Factor Archetypes. She is the Archetype of compassion, the epitome of all that the goddess Kwan Yin represents. Oozing delightful Mother Theresa energy, she is the first one to say yes when someone or something is in need. A champion of causes, Advocate Rescuer will throw herself at the things she believes in most. All of them. They could be callings to support people, animals, the environment or all three. She can find someone or something needing help often before the person or cause realises, they are in need. This is one of her innate gifts and strengths and how she expresses this matters significantly.

Deeply feeling, she is a sensitive soul who wears her heart on her sleeve, available for all who need it, even when they do not know they do. She is open, vulnerable, deeply feeling, an emotional being who is sensitive. The Advocate Rescuer, like all 12 Thrive Factor Archetypes, is present in every woman. She may not actively be part of your Thrive Factor profile, but she exists within you in some way. She is the part of you who feels the pain and suffering of the world. She is the part of you who gives generously of your time to the things, people and causes that matter, that are important to you. She is the part of you who throws herself in before being asked. She is the part of you who is kind and caring and wants to make a difference for those you believe cannot do so for themselves. She is the part of you who donates – time, money, resources, emotion – to anyone or anything you perceive to be in need.

She is also the part of you who runs herself ragged. The part of you who says yes too often and then has regrets when you realise how little time you have to get everything done. She is the part of you who says "well I had to do it because no one else would!" and who also says "no one ever says thank you for everything I do!" and "I'm never saying yes again, no one was grateful for ALL the time and effort I put in!" She is the part of you who finds yourself stretched way too thin. Trying to be in too many places at once. Resenting that you said you would help. Feeling bad because you feel resentful. Worrying what others will think if and when you say no. Believing no one will value you unless you keep saying yes. She is the part of you with a big, open heart that others do appreciate and come to rely on. Take this as the gift it is. You are valued, appreciated and important to so many. Celebrate that beautiful, sensitive soul.

the advocate rescuer's greatest gift to give herself is self-advocacy

What is self-advocacy?

- It is being clear about what you want and need
- It is self-acknowledgment – acknowledging yourself instead of expecting others to
- It is speaking up and saying no when you know that is right – for you
- It is saying yes to you first
- It is acknowledging you are sensitive, emotional and that everything you do does come from a good place
- It is celebrating your strengths and being aware of your potential challenges
- It is pausing before jumping in to help and asking, "does this person or cause really need me or am I diving in as a rescuer?"
- It is choosing YOU as a priority, not an afterthought.

advocate rescuer and self celebration

With your big heart and overwhelming desire to say yes and throw yourself into the ring to help, even before or without being asked, every Advocate Rescuer within can be terrible with self celebration.

This month, to honour the parts of you that are

Kind, Compassionate, Helpful, Big hearted, Generous, Supportive and Caring

This is your invitation to spend time taking care of yourself in ways that feel like you're saying yes to you!

Being an advocate for herself is something your inner Advocate Rescuer is wise to learn. It's not always the easiest thing for an Advocate Rescuer to do. It is possibly not the easiest thing for you to do either, whether you are an Advocate Rescuer or not.

- You find yourself juggling demands from every direction
- You find yourself fulfilling so many roles
- You find yourself saying yes even when your heart says no
- You find yourself wanting to please
- You find yourself wanting to be nice, kind, generous.

You find yourself screaming from the inside "I can't do another thing for someone else" even though the words you hear come out of your mouth are "yes, sure, how can I help?" or "where do you want me to be and when.." or "of course I'll do that for you!"

to celebrate yourself is to

- Get clear on what you want and need and to ask for it
- To expect your wishes to be respected and responded to
- To learn to say no more than you say yes to others. Saying yes all the time to external requests is a form of saying no to you
- Take time to nourish your emotional, sensitive heart
- Rest often
- Give to yourself first
- Ask others before rushing in to do things for them
- Acknowledge yourself instead of seeking external validation
- Show kindness to yourself
- See your sensitivities as strengths instead of the parts of you that are broken or the parts of you that make others unsure of your generosity
- Have strong boundaries that support you
- Have a giving fund – one that has banks of time, money and emotions.

reflection prompts

One way to gain insight into who you are and to tune into the parts of you to be celebrated – and there are a lot of them! – is to do active reflection. These prompts could be used as a theme for journaling, for meditation, for an art practice, or as a discussion topic with a friend. This month, the first in your year of self celebration, declare regular time in your schedule for active reflection.

The Advocate Rescuer brings reflection to how self compassionate you are

She offers you an opportunity for inner connection to your voice, your heart and your desire to do good in the world, supporting yourself and others. The Advocate Rescuer is innately wired to care for others before herself which is something many women identify with. The Advocate Rescuer in all of us will be better off for caring for herself first.

If you know your Thrive Factor Archetypes and know you are an Advocate Rescuer, pay extra attention to these reflection prompts. Use them any time you're feeling the need to rush out and help the world. Use them when you're craving recognition. Use them to nurture your sensitive heart. If you don't yet know your Archetypes or are unsure if you are an Advocate Rescuer you can still benefit from these reflections. We each have parts of all 12 Thrive Factor Archetypes within us, so a month of Advocate Rescuer inspired reflections will be glorious for you.

- Am I being an advocate in this situation or am I feeling a strong desire to fix things?
- What is the need I am trying to fulfil which makes me feel so compelled to jump right in and help?
- Is what I am doing healthy for me, my family, my clients, and those I care about the most?
- What cause am I most passionate about and how can I volunteer a balanced portion of my time to support it or them?
- What do I need to remember is most important for me before I say yes to someone or something I feel compelled to help?
- How can I create more self-balance in my life rather than feeling caught between all the directions my compassionate heart is being pulled in?
- What do I have to forgive myself for? Am I willing to forgive myself? How will I forgive myself?
- Before I say yes, what do I need to consider so I know I am making the best decision and taking the best course of action for everyone involved, including me?
- Are my relationships healthy?
- How can I give myself the compassion I easily give others?
- What does self compassion mean to me?

afformations

The Advocate Rescuer's afformations are designed to expand self compassion, open to self support and to guide you to self acknowledgement. Working with afformations creates expansion and a dynamic that opens you to experience even more celebration. When you ask the right questions and get playful with discovering answers for them, anything is possible. Afformations are fabulous for journaling, visualisation or meditation prompts or simply for reflecting.

- **What if the way I genuinely help was something people appreciated?**
- **What if my compassion was core to my marketing message?**
- **What if I was loved and appreciated each day?**
- **What if I already had supportive boundaries?**
- **What if my ability to be kind and caring positively contributed to my wealth and abundance in a compassionate way?**
- **What if compassion was my superpower?**
- **What if I already had all the recognition I needed?**
- **What if I could easily expand into self kindness, self love to find self celebration fun and exciting?**
- **You could create more afformations of your own to embrace the Advocate Rescuer themes.**

creative exercise

Create a Self-Celebration Ritual with the themes of Self Advocacy, Self Compassion and Self Support Boundaries

A ritual is something you do on a regular basis. It can be anything and personally, I love including things in my rituals that help me feel fabulous. You can't thrive if you're not feeling all the good feels. With our focus on self-celebration your ritual can be filled with things that make you feel good. Words, actions, practices that nourish your heart and support self-advocacy.

Consider the reflections and the afformations you have worked with this month as inspiration.
You could ask these questions for greater clarity.

- What have I learned about myself?
- What nourishes my kind heart?
- What feels like I am being self-compassionate?
- What is a boundary?
- Where in my life do I need to speak up for me?
- What boundaries are important for me to have in place to support me to be me?

your creative exercise invitation

Create a ritual to affirm your self support boundaries by working with the themes of self-advocacy and self-compassion.

Open to a new page in your journal. Write down as many things as you can think of that feel kind and caring. Remember, the focus for this first month is self compassion, closely followed by self advocacy and with a dash of getting clear on the kind of boundaries you need to support you to thrive.

Once you have a page full of awesome options

- Choose one thing that supports you to love yourself more, that's self compassion.
- Choose one thing that supports you to speak up for what you want and need, that's self advocacy.
- Choose one thing that supports you to assert a boundary that supports you to be more you.

The next thing is to choose how frequently you will do these things. I'd love to see you choose to do them daily for an entire month (or longer!) but if this feels out of your comfort zone then aim for two or three times a week. If you miss a day or one of the times you planned to enjoy your ritual, embrace self compassion and start fresh the next day or next time! That is the loving way to support yourself this month.

Thrive Tip: once you've chosen your three ritual activities, schedule time in your diary to actually do them.

ADVOCATE RESCUER
SELF-CELEBRATION CHART

this month I...

Said YES to me	★★★★☆
Reaffirmed my boundaries	★★☆☆☆
Gave more to me than others	★★★☆☆
Reflected on how amazing I am	★☆☆☆☆
Took time out of the busyness to rest	★★★☆☆
Gave myself a gift	★☆☆☆☆
Acknowledged how incredible I am	★★★☆☆
Spoke up for what I want and need	★★★★☆
Said NO to things that don't support me	★★☆☆☆
Refrained from jumping in to rescue someone	★★☆☆☆

Sign up for a year of Bragaudacious self celebration at www.thethrivefactor.com/bragaudacious

self-celebration from around the world

"Learning to celebrate my achievements no matter how big or small has taught me to be more present in my life and my business. One of my favourite ways to celebrate is a dinner out with my soul sisters with whom I can share my successes. At the end of each week, I sit down with my journal and give thanks for all that I have to celebrate"

 Thrive Factor Coach, Kerryn Slater, Philip Island, Victoria, Australia

"Celebration for me is a time of reflection.....so I love to treat myself to a new journal or new book, and then set aside some specific time to sit back read, and immerse myself in my new gift to myself. This is normally in my favourite chair accompanied by a soothing tea or glass of bubbles!"

 Narelle Weir, Perth, WA, Australia

"The one way I love to celebrate, particularly when it comes to business celebrations like signing a new dream client, achieving an income milestone or celebrating a client win is to have a mini dance party with my young children! I get the news, jump up and down, thank the Universe out loud and turn the music up. My kids absolutely love it and now when they experience their own achievements love to do the same thing"

 Tara Hewson, Melbourne, Victoria, Australia

"I celebrate by doing things that make me feel good! This could be spending time with the people I love, pampering myself with a nice massage or pedicure or taking time off and being out in nature. It's all about doing something that brings me joy and keeps me in that state of happiness and high vibration"

 Jen Gutfriend, Alberta, Canada

Month Two
HEROINE ADVENTURER

archetype themes

Bravery, Adventure, Determination, Focus, Nature, Movement, Gentleness

goddess inspiration

Artemis/Dianna

This month we take inspiration from the Heroine Adventurer, the second of the 12 Thrive Factor Archetypes. She is the Archetype of adventure. She's always up for pushing the boundaries and stretching the limits, for herself and others. She doesn't settle for mediocrity in any way.

A defender of women and children, she champions causes supporting these members of society, particularly when she senses they are in a vulnerable space and need support. She uses her voice and drive to create support networks and solutions to help those she believes in the most. She's incredibly loyal and that loyalty extends to everyone – individual through to organisation - she believes in.

She can be so focused and tenacious that her self care and balance between work and play can easily swing one way or the other. When focused on a goal she can become blinkered, tuning out all distractions, including people and things she says are important to her. In these times her loved ones, friends, colleagues, clients can easily feel neglected. Her tenacity is to be admired, but it can also be her achilles heel.

Nature is the antidote to her fierce focus and over commitment to achieving. It balances her hustle vibe so beautifully. Spending time outdoors is essential. Her adventurous spirit wants to climb mountains, swim oceans, hike across remote regions, climb trees, workout every day and conquer goals every step of the way. Nothing small and easy for the Heroine Adventurer. Go all in to win or don't bother at all can be her mantra at times.

While a walk at her local park or along the beachfront, or the winding path in the trees at her local nature reserve is a fabulous balancer in her daily life, time away in the depths of the kind of nature that nourishes her is required frequently. Feet on the earth, in the water. Hugging a tree, showing her face to the sun, dancing in the rain. All equalising in the best possible way for this soul.

The Heroine Adventurer, as you learned with the Advocate Rescuer is, like all 12 Thrive Factor Archetypes, present in every woman. She may not actively be part of your Thrive Factor profile, but she exists within you in some way. She is the part of you who gets competitive about what she wants. She is the part of you who loves the great outdoors and adventure.

She is the part of you who can focus and put all her energy into making change for herself and others. She is tenacious, bold, expansive and has a can-do attitude all of the time. She is also the part of you who can do too much, forget to rest, ignore the signs that your health isn't your focus. She is the part of you who over works, plays hard and can struggle to find the balance and calm amongst the chaos of life and living boldly and in full colour.

She is the part of you who finds yourself wanting the very best, striving to achieve as an ambitious woman who is proud to claim she has goals and a desire to experience success. Draw on her independence, her determination, her gift of focus and her ability to fiercely defend what matters most. Take her strength, her love of moving her body and her desire to adventure as reminders you too have these qualities. Gratefully use her undeniable energy to back herself and what she deeply desires. Connect to her love of nature and her need for self care, compassion, and kindness, given to herself as a priority. Spend time with animals, another great love of hers, and pay attention to the gifts they have to offer. Presence, simplicity, connection, a desire to belong as opposed to being so independent and walking the path of life alone.

the heroine adventurer's greatest gift to give herself is self-care

What is self-care?

- It is combining rest into your days as an equal priority to your work time
- It is doing things that nourish you from the inside out
- It is letting go of the need to win and enjoying experiencing in the moment, being truly present with yourself and others
- It is being kind to yourself
- It is indulging in things you'd previously judge as frivolous or unnecessary because they were feminine, soft skills, emotive, not powerful
- It is releasing the need to hustle and understanding doing less could be your most productive state to be in
- It is choosing YOU as a priority, not an afterthought.

heroine adventurer and self celebration

With your tenacious focus and determined desire to achieve, often to the detriment of your personal wellbeing, every Heroine Adventurer within can be resistant to self celebration.

This month, to honour the parts of you that are

Focused, Adventurous, Caring, Compassionate, Achieving,
Present and Feminine

This is your invitation to spend time taking care of yourself in ways that feel like you're truly caring for you!

Being a nourishing champion for herself is something your inner Heroine Adventurer will be wise to learn. It's not always the easiest thing for a Heroine Adventurer to do. It is possibly not the easiest thing for you to do either, whether you are a Heroine Adventurer or not.

- You find yourself falling into hustle as a default
- You find yourself letting self care fall to the wayside because of the enticement of achieving
- You find yourself resisting rest because you believe doing more is the only way
- You find yourself craving things you judge as not who you are
- You find yourself wanting to find balance, to give, to be supported, to enjoy the moments.

You find yourself saying (often only to yourself for fear of being considered weak or not successful enough) "I just want to be happy with what I already have" even though the words you hear come from your inner drive are saying "keep focused" or "you can do this, it's who you are to be a success" or "rest, bahahahah, that's for the weak!"

to celebrate yourself is to

- Understand your drive to achieve and honour that with compassion
- Create space for regular self care
- Learn that doing less truly can amplify your productivity
- Take time to nourish yourself from every angle – body, mind, spirit, soul
- Acknowledge what you already have accomplished
- Celebrate your wins with a gentleness that shows they matter to you and are not just another accomplishment to add to your metaphorical winner's board
- Allow yourself to be supported
- Give gratefully to the things that matter to you
- Drop the pretences and shields and let the vulnerable parts of yourself shine
- Indulge in things that feel feminine and frivolous
- Let go of whatever you are fixated on
- Reprioritise what matters to you most.

reflection prompts

One way to gain insight into who you are and to tune into the parts of you to be celebrated – and there are a lot of them! – is to do active reflection. These prompts could be used as a theme for journaling, for meditation, for an art practice, or as a discussion topic with a friend or group of friends. This month, the second in your year of self celebration, continue to create regular time in your schedule for active reflection.

It is such a nourishing gift for all women to do in ways that honour who she innately is in the world. Each Thrive Factor Archetype has her own ways to reflect. Engaging with the monthly reflection prompts will provide you with insight into how you can use each Archetype to support wholistic reflection so as to gain insight and, if it arises, make choices and take action in line with what makes sense and you know is best for you.

The Heroine Adventurer brings reflection to how self caring you actually are

She offers you opportunity for inner connection to your focus, your determination, your desire to achieve and also to your desire to champion women and children, animals and nature. The Heroine Adventurer is innately wired to experience achievement in the world, something that is not always acknowledged by women. You have ambition. The Heroine Adventurer in all of us will be better off for acknowledging that and drawing attention to how to honour that ambition and drive to live life fully.

If you know your Thrive Factor Archetypes and know you are a Heroine Adventurer, pay extra attention to these reflection prompts. Use them any time you're feeling the need to push, hustle and over exert yourself to win, to achieve, to prove yourself in the world. Use them when you're craving understanding. Use them to nurture your adventurous heart. If you don't yet know your Archetypes or are unsure if you are a Heroine Adventurer you can 100% benefit from these reflections. We each have parts of all 12 Thrive Factor Archetypes within us, so a month of Heroine Adventurer inspired reflections will be nourishing for you.

- What sort of adventure or journey will fulfill me the most and enable me to be happy and grateful for who I am, all parts of me included?

- What type of physical activity or movement makes me feel fantastic, expansive, adventurous and full of energy?

- How can I create balance to ensure I fulfill my need for adventure whilst staying engaged and grounded in the real and present world I exist in day to day?

- How can I allow myself to ask for help or let others help me when I need assistance rather than feeling I have to do everything myself - usually because I can?

- How can I release my need for independence, which often comes at the cost of my long term wellbeing?

- How can I use my determination and focus in my business, whilst staying open and aware of the bigger picture and other people and things around me?

- What sort of boundaries do I hide behind or allow to stop me from moving forward and accomplishing the awesome things I dream of experiencing and having in my business and in my life?

- Are the boundaries I have in my life healthy for me? Or do they enable me to hide or avoid? It is better for my wellbeing to be out in the open and vulnerable, connected, and able to say yes to the support that I am offered!

- How can I shed the layers, boundaries, and armour I have in place, trusting I will be safe and welcomed as my true self without these things?

- What do I stand to achieve by shedding what no longer serves me?

- What place does independence have in my business and life and how does it positively support and help me?

- What can I do to practice self-care on a regular basis?

- What is self care for me?

- Who do I desire to support in the world and how can I turn my focus, fierceness, and determination towards supporting this cause, community, group or person?

- Where in nature do I feel most alive and free, energised?

- How can I bring that experience into my life on a more frequent basis, to fully reap the benefit?

afformations

The Heroine Adventurer's afformations are designed to expand self care, open to resting and doing less and to guide you to express self gratitude and discover the power in being gentle. Working with afformations creates expansion and a dynamic that opens you to experiencing even more celebration. When you ask the right questions and get playful with discovering answers for them, anything is possible. Afformations are fabulous for journaling, visualisation or meditation prompts or simply for reflecting.

- **What if turning my determined, fierce focus inward to create gentleness was nourishing?**
- **What if my adventurous spirit was energising and freeing?**
- **What if I my greatest accomplishments came from honouring the power within my feminine expression?**
- **What if I had enthusiasm for resting more?**
- **What if engaging with nature was my go to each day?**
- **What if I achieved significantly more by doing less?**
- **What if I already had all the accomplishments I needed?**
- **What if I could easily expand into self care, self gratitude and find self celebration motivating?**
- **You could create more afformations of your own to embrace the Heroine Adventurer themes.**

creative exercise

Create an Honouring Self Care Practice with the themes of Self Love, Self Acceptance and Self Adventure

An honouring self care practice is such a beautiful gift to give yourself. It is also a gift you give to others by leading by example. The Heroine Adventurer loves to be a leader, at the forefront of things, so this will be a brilliant way to express her and nourish you at the same time.

When I use the term self care and practice together, I encourage you to truly see this as a practice. It can become something not to achieve at, but to immerse yourself in for the sake of experience, for the sake of letting go and for the sake of unlearning unhealthy hustle behaviours that have driven you to exist with an underpinning of have to, must do, should do, it's essential to do in order to achieve whatever you have your sights set on.

Before defining your honouring self care practice take some time to get clear on what self care and self honour mean to you. You can journal to create this understanding or try something else that you either know works for you, or that you'd like to try. The Heroine Adventurer is Ms Adventure after all.

I find journaling, visualising, meditation, drawing things in my journal (honouring my Visionary Creator Archetype), chatting with inspiring (probably Inspirer Believers) friends and reflective practices all useful and I choose what feels best in the moment to create the space and energy
for insight that I seek.

- **What does self care mean to me?**
- **What makes me feel nourished?**
- **What makes me feel pressured?**

- **What would I let go of if I felt I could?**
- **What could honouring myself look and feel like?**
- **What energises and motivates me?**
- **How much time can and will I dedicate to self care?**
- **Is there anything else about self care do I want to include in this reflection?**

Don't forget to consider what the Heroine Adventurer inspired afformations have offered you in this reflection.

your creative exercise invitation

Every woman can benefit from understanding what self care is and weaving more of it into her days, weeks, months and years. I often imagine how nourished and truly engaged with the world we would all be with more self care.

This wonder comes from years of denying myself the kind of self care I now understand is essential. I don't have the Heroine Adventurer Archetype, this was driven by the combination of my Visionary Creator, Liberator Engineer and Mentor Teacher.

They are an over achieving trio when you have them together in your Thrive Factor profile. I laugh with compassion at them now when they get all "let's hustle!" Nope ladies. Let's chill more and create space, rest and nourishment for the betterment of all. And with that I book another float tank session!

Your gift of a creative invitation this month is to create a practice to affirm and honour self care in your life, work, business - in every aspect of you being you. Take your previous reflection as inspiration and motivation and consider doing something that feels so out of character for you.

Perhaps it has been something you have always wanted to try.

Perhaps it is something that feels so indulgent it's always been something you have resisted. The more indulgent the better!

Make a list of options and across the month of the Heroine Adventurer, choose at least one a week. When you find the things that nourish you the most, continue to create time and space for them. Self care is, as I mentioned previously, a practice and it is a practice to enjoy, not to turn into a chore. The more you let go and allow yourself to experience self care with the support of self acceptance and self adventure, the better everything could be for you, for those that matter to you, for all.

Thrive Tip: making self care a daily practice can change your entire day, no matter what rises up in the day. Schedule 5 minutes a day to experience self care in a way that nourishes you

HEROINE ADVENTURER
SELF-CELEBRATION CHART

this month I...

Took plenty of time to rest by letting go of the hustle	★★★★
Spent abundant time in nature	★★
Included the important people in the things that matter	★★★
Connected with a group or cause that is important to me	★
Shared my wins proudly	★★★
Let someone help me with something	★
Acknowledged how tenacious I am	★★★
Enjoyed time with the animals in my life	★★★★
Let others feel a sense of winning	★★
Paused to reflect before setting another goal or throwing myself into doing more	★★

Sign up for a year of Bragaudacious self celebration at www.thethrivefactor.com/bragaudacious

self-celebration from around the world

"My motto is YOU'RE ALLOWED!
Celebration comes when you experience the freedom of being allowed to go where you flow.
I ate a salad in the bath last night. Why? Because I'm allowed.
I'm allowed to be over the top excited about the non-profit I'm building.
You're allowed to buy the ridiculously expensive shoes because they make you feel sexy.
You're allowed to sing at the top of your lungs while everyone is watching.
When you realize that you never have to hide who you are, celebration becomes as easy as breathing."

 Jesika Liston, Great Falls Montana, US

"Celebration energy is so powerful for me. It beautifully mixes the deliciousness of gratitude, love, excitement, abundance, purpose and joy. So, when I choose to celebrate, I go all-in with my mind, body and Soul.

I THINK and say words that light me up, like: "Woohooo! Yay! Thank you, thank you, thank you! This is AMAZING. I am amazing! I love it!"

I FEEL the energy in my body - the vibrations and sensations. The warmth, the tingling, the dance of energy within me and on my skin. And I breathe into these powerful vibrations and notice them expanding, increasing, intensifying.

I OBSERVE my mind and body's joy as they centre themselves in their celebration - knowing that life is unfolding exactly as it's meant to, always in my highest good. Yep - I love CHOOSING to celebrate. The big, the small, the all."

 Jo Naughton, Nottinghamshire, UK

"Until a few years ago, I took great pride in getting lots of sh*t done, all the time, regardless of anything else. I was a machine. People would literally ask me how I got so much done. I had a thriving business, two children under 2, a decent-sized house that always seemed pretty tidy and welcoming, I had a fabulous social life and I prioritised Me Time and looked after myself pretty well. But one thing I never did was make time to reflect, review, take stock and high-five myself for everything I was achieving. A textbook Virgo (coupled with being a Queen Ruler and Mentor Teacher) meant my to do list was never-ending (just the way I liked it) and my priority was to tick-and-flick as many tasks as humanly possible. There was no room for celebration. And that got pretty damn boring.

I also (begrudgingly) require Words Of Affirmation (one of my top Love Languages) and at some point came to realise that a lot of my doing was, in actual fact, me seeking external validation and approval. The more I became aware of that, the more I started to celebrate my wins; at first internally, then with my nearest-and-dearest, and eventually with anyone who'd listen. I'd always been a champion of other people celebrating themselves and perpetually frustrated by those who didn't (or, even worse, those who were super self-critical - ugh!) so I ate some humble pie and started practicing what I preach. And as soon as I did, it was like a little door opened for the people around me and they started experimenting with it too. Now I ADORE how we can all blow our own trumpets - unapologetically - and celebrate how f'ing awesome we are!"

 Claire Riley, Gold Coast, QLD, Australia

Month Three
INSPIRER BELIEVER

archetype themes

Inspiration, Energy, Expansion, Intuition, Intensity, Expression

goddess inspiration

Brigid

This month we take inspiration from the Inspirer Believer, the third of the 12 Thrive Factor Archetypes. She is the Archetype of inspiration. She's always up for being inspired and sharing what inspires her, often with intense excitement and an energy that is palpable but not always sustainable. A cheerleader for anyone she is inspired by the goddess Brigid, muse of all who freely gives of her energy to beliefs, people and experiences that motivate and inspire her. This can often be at the cost of her personal energy reserves which can impact her personal motivation, enthusiasm, and inspiration in a magnitude of ways. Understanding how to preserve her energy is a lesson that can take some time to master. Learning to pay attention to the signs that tell her that her energy is being drained and pausing responsively to re-energise will be a great support to the Inspirer Believer.

She has a beautiful and humble way of engaging with others and tends to trust openly and abundantly due to her in built belief people are good. She can feel incredibly disappointed when her trust, her support, her cheering, her inspiration are not respected. This can drain her energy in an instant and leave her wondering why she bothers at all. She has a fragile heart and spends her life learning things that can, if she allows them to, expand her sense of resilience. This will serve her well.

Along with a belief that people are good, until proven otherwise, this optimistic realist woman is also a gifted potentialist. She sees the potential in people and has a huge desire for them to see it in themselves. She is most inspired by those who follow a calling to bring their innate potential to life.

How they do it is not the focus, the fact they have excites and energises the Inspirer Believer. If you have an Inspirer Believer in your world, you will know it. She is the greatest and loudest cheerleader for all she believes in – family, friend, child, colleagues, strangers on the internet. It takes a lot for her to lose faith in others but when she does it can be a no turning back situation.

While she shares how inspirational she wants to be, accepting she already is the inspiration she wishes to be can be something Inspirer Believer struggles with. She humbly turns away compliments and feedback received that affirms she is motivating, inspiring and someone others aspire to be like. It is not that she feels awkward receiving this feedback, she simply takes a while to see and celebrate this reality. Her greatest gift to herself is to be inspired by who she is, what she is creating and what she is sharing with the world.

The Inspirer Believer, as you learned with the previous Archetypes is, like all 12 Thrive Factor Archetypes, present in every woman. She may not actively be part of your Thrive Factor profile, but she exists within you in some way. She is the part of you who gets fired up and energised when she experiences things that inspire her. She is the part of you guided by strong beliefs and core understandings that support you to make sense of your place in the world. She is your enthusiasm, motivation, drive and belief in the good of people, even when you have experienced being let down or worse still, burned by others or burned yourself out. She is also the part of you who can over give, over support, over cheer. The part of you who gets carried away and is all or nothing when a new belief or concept or experience takes hold and speaks to you with inspiration. She is the part of you who wants to give up when you are tired and forgets that rest and re-energising activities are essential for your wellbeing.

She is the part of you who finds yourself seeking inspiration externally and slowly recognising the magic and energy that comes from the inspiration she finds within. Draw on her energy and her beliefs to support you, becoming your own cheerleader, one you can always rely on. Take her belief in others and her belief in innate potential and let this nurture your belief in humanity. Use her undeniable energy to tap into motivation and enthusiasm to act on inspiration freely and with gratitude and belief. Connect to her inner fire and let it guide you forward to be the most expressive inspirational you, you dream to be.

the inspirer believer's greatest gift to give herself is self inspiration

What is self inspiration?

- It is pausing to acknowledge the impact you have already created
- It is doing things that fire you up with sustained energy
- It is recognising the significance of the beliefs that guide your every move in the world
- It is being gentle with yourself in times of low energy
- It is remembering the bigger picture and impact you wish to make, particularly in times of low mood or energy that leaves you feeling hopeless – this will pass!
- It is having gratitude for seeing the good in others and being able to action your boundaries when your abundance of support and cheering is not respected
- It is celebrating YOU as the inspiration you already are in the world.

inspirer believer and self celebration

With your high energy excitement to share inspiration, often leading to extremes of energy highs and lows, every Inspirer Believer within can be resistant to self celebration.

This month, to honour the parts of you that are

Energised, Inspiring, Excitable, Intuitive, Creative, Emotive and Fiery

This is your invitation to spend time taking care of yourself in ways that feel like you're truly caring for you!

Being an energised women in flow for yourself is something your inner Inspirer Believer will be wise to learn. It's not always the easiest thing for an Inspirer Believer to do. It is possibly not the easiest thing for you to do either, whether you are a Inspirer Believer or not.

- You find yourself feeling burnt out by giving too much
- You find yourself mistrusting your instincts when they tell you to balance your enthusiasm and cheerleading with rest and renewal
- You find yourself uncertain about your ability to create sustained energy
- You find yourself desiring to be inspired and ignore how inspirational you actually are
- You find yourself wanting to trust yourself, others, your intuition and your inspiration but still question this trust.

You find yourself saying (often only to yourself for fear of being considered un-inspirational) "I want to have all the energy I need to be me in the world" even though the words you hear come from your intuition are saying "you are an inspiration" or "energy is always available to you" or "your fire is your power!"

to celebrate yourself is to

- Understand that you are pure inspiration to those around you
- Create space for rest and energy nourishment
- Learn to say no when your energy is low or compromised
- Take time to engage with gentle things that fire up your inspiration but don't overwhelm you energetically
- Acknowledge how valued you are already
- Celebrate your impact, it is so powerful and energising
- Allow yourself to follow your instincts, you can't deny the energy that inspired action offers
- Give gratitude to all you are, all you create and all you share in the world
- Be inspired by you!
- Indulge in whatever energises and balances your enthusiasm and fire with gentleness and calm
- Let go of whatever you have decided makes you anything but the inspiration you seek to be
- Reprioritise the way you work and share by coming home to the beliefs that support you.

reflection prompts

As you have possibly read by now in other chapters, one way to gain insight into who you are and to tune into the parts of you to be celebrated – and there are so many of them! – is to do active reflection. These prompts could be used as a theme for journaling, for meditation, for an art practice, or as a discussion topic with a friend. This month, the second in your year of self celebration, continue to create regular time in your schedule for active reflection.

It is such a nourishing and expansive gift for all women to do in ways that honour who you innately are in the world. Each Thrive Factor Archetype has her own ways to reflect. Engaging with the monthly reflection prompts will provide you with insight into how you can use this months Archetype to support wholistic reflection so as to gain insight and, if it arises, make choices and take action in line with what makes sense and you know is best for you.

The Inspirer Believer brings reflection to how self inspirational you truly are

She offers you opportunity for inner connection to your energy, motivations, inspirations, fiery enthusiasm, belief systems and also to your desire to be an inspiration for others. The Inspirer Believer is innately wired to experience and create inspiration in the world, something that is often dismissed by women. You are inspiring, whether you recognise and celebrate that fact or not. All women are. Inspirer Believer women are simply inspirational on a whole other level. The true cheerleaders of the world. The Inspirer Believer in all of us will be better off for acknowledging this and drawing attention to how to honour your desire to be and reality you are an inspiration so as to live life fully and totally thriving.

If you know your Thrive Factor Archetypes and know you are a Inspirer Believer, pay extra attention to these reflection prompts. Use them any time you're feeling the need to retreat, feel disappointed, let down by an experience or person, get fired up and sense you are burning yourself out. Use them when you're craving energy. Use them to nurture your inspiration heart that believes so freely in the good of others, even when they forget that they are or can be inherently good in the world.

If you don't yet know your Archetypes or are unsure if you are an Inspirer Believer you can 100% benefit from these reflections. We each have parts of all 12 Thrive Factor Archetypes within us, so a month of Inspirer Believer inspired reflections will certainly be encouraging and motivating for you.

- **How can I inspire others more without depleting my valuable personal energy?**
- **In what ways do I inspire others?**
- **How can I continue to inspire myself frequently and appreciate the inspiration I radiate into the world?**
- **How can I use my personal beliefs to truly support me to achieve my goals and dreams?**
- **What are my favourite quotes, sayings, memes, and motivations and how can I use them to add more positive energy into my life? (and as an added benefit of sharing them I'll be inspiring others too)**
- **What inspires me and how does it inspire me?**
- **How can I share more of what inspires me in my work, business and in my life?**
- **How can I remember to be inspired by myself and accept that I am inspirational and that being so is a fabulous and energising reality?**

- What am I currently committed to that drains me or makes me feel challenged and exhausted? What can I do to change that?

- How can I express my fiery side - the part of me that others would call my excitable or overly enthusiastic side - in a way that is healthy and doesn't lead me to lose my temper, get frustrated, burn out or become ferociously fierce and defensive?

- How can I stay motivated and supportive when I feel challenged or threatened? Of myself? Of others?

- What steps can I take each day to stay grounded in my body, connected to my heart and able to listen rationally to my head?

- How can I better trust my instincts about someone and give myself permission to walk away when I intuitively know the right thing for me to do is to remove myself for the situation and whatever relationship we have?

- What things do I know help me to regain my mojo when it has gone A.W.O.L?

- How do I know I have abundant energy?

- How can I sustain that energy in a state of flow instead of the extremes it can be?

afformations

The Inspirer Believer's afformations are designed to expand self inspiration, opening you to trust your intuition and to guide you to express the inspiration you are for all who have the honour of being in your life – personally and professionally. Working with afformations creates expansion and a dynamic that opens you to experiencing even more celebration. When you ask the right questions and get playful with discovering answers for them, anything is possible. Afformations are fabulous for journaling, visualisation or meditation prompts or simply for reflecting.

- **What if my energy was sustainable and accessible anytime I needed it?**
- **What if I was already the inspiration I desire to be?**
- **What if I could trust my instincts and intuition in every situation?**
- **What if it was a good thing to rest to renew?**
- **What if believing in others was one of my superpowers?**
- **What if I could create supportive boundaries that protected my energy and allowed me to be present in the world?**
- **What if I cheered myself before others?**
- **What if my inspiration rippled out into the world effortlessly because I choose to be inspired by myself, what I am creating and what I am sharing as a priority?**
- **You could create more afformations of your own to embrace the Inspirer Believer themes.**

creative exercise

The Fire Within with the themes of Self Inspiration, Self Belief and Self Motivation

Every woman has an inner fire and recognising and celebrating it is most definitely an ideal way to celebrate the energy of the Inspirer Believer. As an Archetype, her inner fire is grounded in the strong beliefs that guide her forward in everything she does. The beliefs will shift, change, and evolve over time, but at the core of each belief she follows is an inner fire sparking her inspiration.

Capturing your fire within is the theme of this month's creative exercise. Inspirer Believer is going to love every day of doing this. The exercise invites you to allow more inspiration into your days, letting the beliefs and energy guide your days with enthusiasm and excitability. It will become a motivating resource when times arise when you feel less energised. An Inspirer Believer can easily forget that her hopeless times can quickly transform. Remembering your inner fire and what makes you inspirational, as well as what energises you, is the most beautiful gift to create for yourself.

your creative exercise invitation

Capturing your inner fire is going to be so fun this month. This exercise has been created for you to connect with your inspiration and sparks of energy that are calling you to express more of yourself.

What you need:

- A large sheet of white or light coloured card or paper
- Paper in flame or fire colours, or any colours that ignite your inspiration – this is your inner fire being expressed
- Glue stick
- Scissors
- A darker coloured pen or marker
- Your wild inspiration
- Trust in your instincts – they have your back sister!

What to do:

1. Use the coloured paper and cut out shapes that are flame shaped – make sure they are large enough to write on
2. Cut out enough shapes for the days of the month
3. Stick the shapes onto the larger piece of card or paper in any design that inspires you
4. Each day add something related to your inner fire, energy and inspiration to one of the flames. You could use the prompts below to get you fired up.

Prompts:

- Today I felt inspired by...
- My energy today was boosted by...
- When I remembered I believe... I felt...
- I feel energised when...
- I get fired up by...
- When my fire is bright I...
- I am most inspired by...
- Today I was told I was inspiring because...

Thrive Tip: Keep your Inspirer Believer creation somewhere easy to see and be motivated by all year round. If you're not able to keep it then take a photo of it and keep it on your phone or computer or print a copy and stick it in your journal.

INSPIRER BELIEVER
SELF-CELEBRATION CHART

this month I...

Nurtured my energy each day	★★★★
Got inspired by motivating people, experiences and things	★★
Trusted my beliefs, even when the trust was challenged	★★★
Allowed myself to feel all my emotions and to connect to my fiery energy	★
Let go of people, things, experiences that drained me	★★★
Nourished myself with new things that energised me	★
Stayed focused on the bigger picture	★★★
Was gentle when I felt my energy wane	★★★★
Allowed myself to rest and reconnect with what matters to me most	★★
Let my inspiration guide me, not define me	★★

Sign up for a year of Bragaudacious self celebration at www.thethrivefactor.com/bragaudacious

self-celebration from around the world

"I make an intentional point to celebrate both big and small victories. It's so easy to think about what's next, but even just a few moments of presence can have a lasting impact. I love to dance and howl to celebrate! Maybe it's because I'm a Taurus (ruled by the throat chakra), but no celebration is complete without a guttural howl! AAARRROOOO!"

 Morgan Garza, Denver, Colorado, United States

"Everyday is a new beginning- a fresh start. Just as the sun rises in the morning and the last evening star bows out as the darkness fades, so too can your worries and your fears.

Yesterday is gone, there's no need to stay there and be lost in the darkness of anger and resentment. Tomorrow isn't here, there's no need to fear it or lose yourself in worry about it. You are here now, Today, in the Present. To wake up and See a new day is a gift in itself…. not everyone gets to do that. It is a true gift- thus why it is The Present.

So like the new day, embrace it with excitement for your new beginnings. Love unconditionally. Laugh spontaneously. Have fun. Take chances. See everything with fresh eyes and have clarity. Keep it simple. Embrace your life and celebrate you, for you are an incredible walking miracle and the World is a better place for having you here"

 Christine Farnham, Merimbula, NSW, Australia

"All of my life's special moments are celebrated with champagne. It's a perfectly acceptable 24/7 beverage which makes it celebration ready at all times. Champagne overflows in abundance and joy. The word effervescence makes me smile, and the bubbles in champagne are a quintessential expression of its magical quality.

My Shapeshifter Alchemist relates to the magic. The pop of a champagne cork is a burst of happiness; an explosion of joy and freedom. My Inspirer Believer is fuelled by that. My Mediator Diplomat often asks if I need to be so indulgent while there are people struggling in the world. But my Advocate Rescuer validates that I need it. That I deserve it. And so the champagne flows as I celebrate life moments that matter. I'm excited by my bubbles-infused path to thriving"

 Trina Sunday, Perth, WA, Australia

"Bubbles, a beautiful meal, manicure/pedicure, shared celebration with friends/family, dance, a getaway, I also keep a record of wins and celebrations as it brings much joy"

 Laura Elkaslassy, Melbourne, Victoria, Australia

".... I feel the edges of my mouth twitch, my whole body tingling from head to toe. I smile and start to move, I open my mouth and break into song, I dance and twirl around with arms held wide to the sky. I wrap my arms around myself in a long strong hug..... This is how I celebrate"

 Fin James, Denmark, WA, Australia

Month Four
LIBERATOR ENGINEER

archetype themes

Freedom, Solutions, Intense Emotion, Capability, Expression, Experience

goddess inspiration

Kali and Pele

This month we take inspiration from the Liberator Engineer, the fourth of the 12 Thrive Factor Archetypes. She is the Archetype of freedom. She's always seeking to create and experience freedom, liberation, and space in all she does and all she creates and believes in.

A rebel who often denies how much she wants to go against the grain, she is innately analytical with a brain wired to make sense of concepts, processes, and frameworks. The Liberator Engineer sees the big picture and understands all the moving parts and how to make them work easily together. This unique talent is something she often under appreciates and others adore! She has a gift for creating solutions that lead to an expansive sense of freedom for herself and others and she adores her driven ability to build outcomes and experiences that others value. She can be a whizz with a spreadsheet and often loves technology for the ease she creates with it.

She is the ultimate freedom weaver and others love having her energy in their space. She can be fun and playful when she feels liberated from whatever has previously limited or held her back. She has a cheeky sense of humour that balances out her tenacity and fierce focus when she's in engineer and builder mode. Call on her when you want to get something done and intensity is required.

Balancing her building and creating energy with the need for space and freedom doesn't always come naturally. You could call her an over achiever, but it is in different ways to this aspect of the Heroine Adventurer and Mentor Teacher Archetypes. When not taking care of her freedom she can find the intense build up of emotion within leading to an implosion which leads to illness, or explosion which can be volcanic. Some may view this as anger, but she really is a peaceful soul when she's letting that emotion release on a regular basis.

If she spends time doing things that nourish her freedom in as many ways as possible, she's contributing to self liberation, something she craves above anything else. It is about simplicity, not complexity. Freedom, not overdoing. Boundaries that weave more freedom into her life, not doling more thinking that will build freedom in. It doesn't. It won't.

The Liberator Engineer, as you learned with the previous three Archetypes is, like all 12 Thrive Factor Archetypes, present in every woman. She may not actively be part of your Thrive Factor profile, but she exists within you in some way. She is the part of you who wants to feel and be free. She is the part of you who can create ease and space in times where she used to feel trapped, overwhelmed and frustrated.

She is also the part of you who can overcomplicate things and transform any experience from feeling free to being complex and contracting. She is the part of you who gets addicted to building and creating and continues to push past her instincts even when they scream at her to pause or completely stop. Listen to that inner voice. It exists for a reason.

She is the part of you who finds yourself able to transform her frustrations into freedom that leads to inspiration and motivation for herself and others. Draw on her rebellious nature and inbuilt depth of emotion that informs her intuition and decision making abilities. Take her analytical and strategic ways of thinking and creating and use these to create your own freedom fuelled life. Gratefully use her sense of space and ease to draw these into your world, creating and experiencing your variations of freedom and liberation while doing so.

the liberator engineer's greatest gift to give herself is self liberation

What is self liberation?

- It is letting go of the things that make you feel trapped or stuck
- It is doing things that create a sense of real and perceived space and expansion
- It is welcoming in people and experiences that expand your thinking, feeling and belief and create action that is liberating for yourself and others
- It is being guided by your innate sense of what freedom is for you
- It is acknowledging the intensity of your emotions and realising everything happens for you and not to you
- It is celebrating your inner rebel and letting her influence you to be, do, have and become totally you
- It is honouring what supports your freedom in all aspects of your life.

liberator engineer and self celebration

With your determination to be free and to use your innate gifts to create freedom at any cost, often to the detriment of your personal liberation, every Liberator Engineer within can be resistant to self celebration.

This month, to honour the parts of you that are

Rebellious, Feeling, Analytical, Liberating, Intense, Freeing and Expansive

This is your invitation to spend time taking care of yourself in ways that feel like you're truly caring for you!

Being a champion for her freedom is something your inner Liberator Engineer is always wise to learn. It's not always the easiest thing for a Liberator Engineer to do. It is possibly not the easiest thing for you to do either, whether you are a Liberator Engineer or not.

- You find yourself falling into complexity
- You find yourself letting rest go because there is always something to build and create
- You find yourself resisting letting go for fear of losing control over the outcome
- You find yourself craving more space, more ease, more freedom
- You find yourself wanting to find opportunities to create freedom for yourself and others all the time and overwhelmed with the enormity of the task.

You find yourself saying (often only to yourself for concern at being labelled unrealistic) "I just want things to be easier" even though the words you hear come from your inner rebel are saying "do more and you'll find your freedom" or "your freedom comes at a cost" or something else unhelpful.

to celebrate yourself is to

- Understand your drive to create freedom
- Create space for yourself in all you do
- Learn that letting go of control and complexity is freedom
- Take time to nourish what supports you to feel greater ease
- Acknowledge your inner rebel and let her have an influence in your life and business/work
- Celebrate your freedom and the effortlessness you already have
- Allow yourself to ask and honour "how can this be easier?"
- Give gratefully to your powerful emotions that are there to guide you
- Drop the frustration that can rise quickly when you don't feel free – this is a significant sign to pay attention to
- Indulge in spaciousness whenever you can
- Let go if it feels like you need to control the outcome
- Reprioritise everything so that freedom comes first – saying no is a power move!

reflection prompts

If you've traversed this book in chapter order you will have seen in other chapters that I have shared how one way to gain insight into who you are and to tune into the parts of you to be celebrated – and there are so many of them! – is to do active reflection. These prompts could be used as a theme for journaling, for meditation, for an art practice, or as a discussion topic with a friend. This month, the second in your year of self celebration, continue to create regular time in your schedule for active reflection.

It is such a nourishing and expansive gift for all women to do in ways that honour who you innately are in the world. Each Thrive Factor Archetype has her own ways to reflect. Engaging with the monthly reflection prompts will provide you with insight into how you can use this month's Archetype to support wholistic reflection so as to gain insight and, if it arises, make choices and take action in line with what makes sense and you know is best for you.

The Liberator Engineer brings reflection to how self liberated and free you truly are

She offers you opportunity for inner connection to your sense of spaciousness, need for freedom, intensity, capability and analytical gifts and also to your desire to be a freedom weaver for others. The Liberator Engineer is innately wired to experience and create freedom, for herself and others. This, like the gifts of the other Thrive Factor Archetypes is something that is often dismissed by women. You are a true liberator, whether you recognise and celebrate that fact or not. All women have the potential to influence their freedom. You do, your friend does, your sister, your colleague, your client, your daughter. Liberator Engineer women are engaging freedom weavers on a whole other level. The true liberators of the world. The Liberator Engineer in all of us will be better off for acknowledging this and drawing attention to how to honour your desire to be and reality you are driven by a need for freedom as much as you need oxygen to breath. This is so as to live life fully and totally thriving.

If you know your Thrive Factor Archetypes and know you are a Liberator Engineer, pay extra attention to these reflection prompts. Use them any time you're feeling the need to break free, to break things before you break down, to define solutions, when you're into analytical mode and overanalysing and over engineering everything, when you crave ease and effortlessness. Use them when you're craving space and freedom. Use them to nurture your liberation fuelled heart that believes every soul deserves to know what it is to be free of whatever real and perceived limits, blocks, restrictions and patterns hold them back.

If you don't yet know your Archetypes or are unsure if you are a Liberator Engineer you can 100% benefit from these reflections. We each have parts of all 12 Thrive Factor Archetypes within us, so a month of Liberator Engineer inspired reflections will certainly be exciting and freeing for you.

- **What actions should I take to clearly see what needs to be done in order to achieve the outcome I am working towards?**

- **How can I liberate myself from what I know is in my way or holding me back?**

- **What tools do I have available to me to build the life I really want to be living?**

- **What systems and supports can I build and rely on to provide the ultimate freedom essential in my business and in my life?**

- **What is the big picture I can see and sense and how do the moving parts work to create ease, effortlessness and freedom for myself and others?**

- What does it mean to me to be and feel completely free?
- How do I bring freedom to others and what lessons can I take from this that I can apply to my own life, work, relationships?
- What is it I really want to say and how can I get my message across in a way that liberates rather than destructs?
- What is the real emotion I am feeling and how can I express myself in a way that is soft and nurturing rather than intense and overwhelming?
- What is the real reason I feel the need to break this down, to change, re-work, tweak, adjust, evolve?
- What is it about this situation that is triggering or activating me to feel like I need to break something?
- What happens when I don't feel free and what signs do I want to act on early to keep the flow of freedom that is so important to me?
- How can I explain to others what is happening when I express my intense emotion? It's important for me to express but I don't want to hurt those around me
- What does ease mean to me?
- What does effortlessness mean to me?
- How can I welcome more ease and effortlessness into my days?
- What things do I love to do because they create a sense of space and expansion?

afformations

The Liberator Engineer's afformations are designed to expand self liberation, opening you to connect with your ability to effortlessly create freedom and to guide you to express the freedom you experience for all who have the honour of being in your life – personally and professionally. Working with afformations creates expansion and a dynamic that opens you to experiencing even more celebration. When you ask the right questions and get playful with discovering answers for them, anything is possible. Afformations are fabulous for journaling, visualisation or meditation prompts or simply for reflecting.

- **What if my need for freedom was something I could effortlessly fulfil each day?**
- **What if freedom was a gift I could share with others?**
- **What if my analytical brain was a source of ease instead of complexity?**
- **What if I started and ended my day feeling spacious?**
- **What if the world around me had all the solutions I desire?**
- **What if my life was already as free as I desire it to be?**
- **What if I could let go of the intense emotion when it made me feel stuck?**
- **What if I could build the life, career, business, relationship I desire and it could be full of the things that support me to be independent, liberated and connected all at once?**
- **You could create more afformations of your own to embrace the Liberator Engineer themes.**

creative exercise

Expanding my Freedom with the themes of Self Liberation, Self Creation, Self Rebellion

Freedom is not limited as a desire to Liberator Engineers. It is a common experience that you hear people talk about often. It might be personal freedom, body freedom, mindset freedom, financial freedom, relationship freedom, freedom in all things. So no matter your Archetypes, this months creative exercise is going to appeal to most of the women reading this. I am sure it'll appeal to you. YAY for more freedom for us all!

It is also a month to tap into your inner rebel. In the past year I have hosted a group coaching experience for women in business, the Rebel Woman mastermind. It has been such a joy to work with women in community and support them as they support each other, by tapping into what makes them authentically unique. I have always seen the rebel within as the woman who chooses herself and let's go of the need to follow the crowds. I have the Liberator Engineer Archetype and my rebel is alive and well and pushing the boundaries a lot of the time. It is not always easy, which goes against the grain of freedom weaving Liberator Engineer, but it has been so worth the experience of honouring my path.

your creative exercise invitation

To create freedom starts with understanding what freedom is for you. So that is the first part of this creative exercise. Spend time connecting with your innate wish for expanded freedom and turn freedom into an avatar, as though she is a person. This is a great way to celebrate the Liberator Engineer Archetype.

Here are prompts to work with to bring your Freedom Avatar to life. Once you have a sense of her read on for the next step in this month's creative exercise.

Freedom avatar prompts:

- If freedom was a person what would she look like?
- What would her hobbies and interests be?
- What colours would she love and why?
- What kind of dress style would appeal to her?
- What matters to her most and why?
- In what ways does she go against the grain, rebelling by being herself?
- What words define her freedom?
- Is there anything else to add?

Ok, it is time to move onto the next phase of this month's creative exercise.

You are invited to create a collage to build a visual representation of your Freedom Avatar.

What you need:

- Old magazines if you have them
- Pictures and words that relate to the aspects of your Freedom Avatar sourced online and printed out
- A large piece of card or paper of any colour that feels freeing to you
- Glue stick
- Scissors
- Your Freedom Avatar description
- A space that is free of clutter so you can spread out as you build your Freedom Avatar collage, just as the Liberator Engineer would do as she is in builder and creator mode.

What to do:

1. Cut out or tear your images so they are free from any backgrounds or inclusions that you don't want on your collage
2. Arrange the images on your large piece of card or paper until the layout feels right to you
3. Begin gluing the pieces in place until they are all where you want them to be
4. Add any additional words or drawing to bring your Freedom Avatar to life.

Thrive Tip: Hang your creation somewhere you can be reminded what freedom means to you and how you can express it beautifully and effortlessly, by being you.

LIBERATOR ENGINEER
SELF-CELEBRATION CHART

this month I...

Focused on feeling and being free in my days	★★★★
Honoured my gift for creating freedom for myself and others	★★
Understood what contributed to a sense of spaciousness and welcomed more	★★★
Let go of the need to change something that didn't need changing	★
Released the intensity and complexity when it arose	★★★
Let myself feel the depth of my emotions and allowed space for them to process	★
Defined what freedom means to me	★★★
Celebrated the newly found ease I have created	★★★★
Choose effortlessness instead of busyness	★★
Did less to achieve more	★★

Sign up for a year of Bragaudacious self celebration at www.thethrivefactor.com/bragaudacious

self-celebration from around the world

"The way that I love to celebrate is through dance!! Every time I have a win or a client has a win - I put on music and Dance, dance, dance. I also have a special money dance that I do when calling in Abundance!!!"

 Victoria Welsh, Indian Rocks Beach, Florida, United States

"As I sat to write something about "how I celebrate" I realised I don't actually have a way of celebrating. In fact, I'm not sure I celebrate enough. I journal in my gratitude diary. Sometimes I might buy myself something, but I don't have a clear and distinct way of actually celebrating. Perhaps because I trust that things just come when there's alignment.

This is a good starting point though, to give this more thought. Perhaps documenting and starting to celebrate my wins with some sort of ritual would be a lovely recognition"

 Angela Sanfilippo, Sydney, NSW, Australia

"How do I celebrate? It's the simple things that satisfy me! A good cup of tea, drunk mindfully. A nourishing meal at a café. A long wander along the beach. A big smile in my heart"

 Louise Carbone, Perth, WA, Australia

"What I started to do to celebrate myself is usually buy a good bottle of champaign and drink it with my lover with a good diner. I make a little speech out loud on what I achieved and what I am celebrating. It truly fills me with joy to honour myself this way"

 Alyson Robinson, Quebec, Canada

Month Five
MEDIATOR DIPLOMAT

archetype themes

Truth, Balance, Listening, Justice, Harmony, Equality, Practical, Pragmatic, Voice

goddess inspiration

Maat

This month we take inspiration from the Mediator Diplomat, the fifth of the 12 Thrive Factor Archetypes. She is the Archetype of balance. She's the Archetype who is focused on creating truth, harmony, justice, and equality for all individuals, and herself.

A woman with the gift of listening to others she does so in a way that those who have her ear feel truly heard. This is an attribute that draws people to her who want to be listened to and wish to have their injustice heard and justified. The thing is, the Mediator Diplomat doesn't always agree, and she can be quick to offer a counter point of view, often upsetting those who had hoped for her support. She says it like it is and can be very black and white about things.

As the truth teller of the 12 Thrive Factor Archetypes, Mediator Diplomat is the litmus for world harmony. She wants to express her truth but doesn't always find this easy to do. That is until she gets fired up when she knows something isn't right. She is the judge of the universe, but not necessarily judgemental. She can be self judgemental and self critical and can have a set of self imposed standards and rules she must abide by. They can be strict and exacting. Her tenacity to set wrongs right and to balance things out in pursuit of harmony makes her the best devil's advocate in any situation. A Mediator Diplomat at the table brings a fresh, practical view to everything.

She can be so determined that everything she creates and shares – all her interactions with her world – need to be value driven and demonstrate quality at every step. This is driven by her inner perfectionist, who can dominate all aspects of her life and cause havoc. Instead of being fixated on everything having to be a certain way, the Mediator Diplomat will benefit so much from understanding she only knows how to create quality things and experiences. So, drop the excessively high standards and judgement that frequently surfaces along with them and focus instead on what you have already experienced and achieved. Gratitude is an antidote to perfectionism.

She is practical and down to earth and as an Archetype, the Mediator Diplomat can be resistant to fun. Her sensible approach to EVERYTHING can mean she misses out on the free expression that can be present in so many other Archetypes. In fact, many women who know they have the Mediator Diplomat in their Thrive Factor Profile have been known to give this Archetype a bad wrap. She is the opposite to the energetic, enthusiastic, big impact Inspirer Believer, for example. But be kind to the Mediator Diplomat parts of you, for they are important and frequently the great leveller of common sense you need to maintain a sense of being grounded and realistic. But do have fun! Mediator Diplomat will expand more into her truth when she is also able to be free with her expression.

The Mediator Diplomat, as you learned with the Archetypes in the previous chapters is, like all 12 Thrive Factor Archetypes, present in every woman. She may not actively be part of your Thrive Factor profile, but she exists within you in some way. She is the part of you who gets sets extreme standards, wants everything to be perfect and just so all the time. She is the part of you who can be judgemental, critical and always balancing things – for yourself and others – in the pursuit of harmony.

She is also the part of you who keeps pushing until she gets things right, by her own standards. She can be self critical and self judgemental, never measuring up to what she believes is needed to be valuable and valued in the world. She benefits from releasing the practical, sensible, pragmatic lenses that are her default and instead allowing in fun and frivolity that don't always show up. If needs be, use other Archetypes to support you to let yourself go a little wild. Go on! You will get so much from doing this for yourself.

the mediator diplomat's greatest gift to give herself is self balance

What is self balance?

- It is understanding what balance truly means for you and taking action to make that your reality
- It is having boundaries with yourself about what and who you listen to
- It is trusting your instincts when something in your gut (or wherever you feel it) says there is a mistruth at play. Always remember you have a fabulously reliable filter for BS when it is around, and you don't have time for that in any form
- It is being considerate of your truth
- It is celebrating when you share your truth with those who matter most to you
- It is releasing the perfectionism and allowing yourself to create and share without the need for things to be a certain way
- It is letting yourself have a little more fun in all the sensible that is generally your default agenda – you have other Archetypes, so let them shine.

mediator diplomat and self celebration

With your quality driven perfectionism and often fixed view of the world, often to the detriment of your personal wellbeing, every Mediator Diplomat within can be resistant to self celebration.

This month, to honour the parts of you that are

Pragmatic, Truthful, Balanced, Aligned, Harmonious,
Quality-driven and Practical

This is your invitation to spend time taking care of yourself in ways that feel like you're truly caring for you!

Being a gentle, balanced soul for herself is something your inner Mediator Diplomat will benefit from learning. It's not always the most effortless thing for a Mediator Diplomat to do. It is possibly not the easiest thing for you to do either, whether you are a Mediator Diplomat or not.

- You find yourself falling into things having to be perfect all the time
- You find yourself holding back from sharing your truths with others based
- on your perception or expectation of being judged
- You find yourself becoming fixed in your view of things, just because you can
- You find yourself arguing to ensure that wrongs are righted, simply to prove a point
- You find yourself seeking to create balance, blending, and aligning all aspects of your life and work, but still feeling out of balance.

You find yourself saying (often only to yourself for concern you may be judged) "I just want to be known for the value I provide" even though the words you hear come from your inner drive are saying "your truth matters" or "you have everything it takes" or "it doesn't need to be perfect to be shared!"

to celebrate yourself is to

- Understand your determination to deliver the most value laden experience

- Create alignment in all you do

- Learn that your truth matters and deserves to be shared

- Relax in your life, letting more ease and less busyness be your new way to be

- Acknowledge what you already have accomplished, with enthusiasm.

- Celebrate all of your accomplishments, instead of focusing on what is still to be completed or could be better

- Allow yourself to be increasingly grateful – gratitude balances perfectionism

- Give your time and an ear only to those who matter to you most

- Honour your gift for listening and know how appreciated this is by others who value being heard in a world that often ignores what they have to say

- Buy yourself things that feel light-hearted, indulgent, flippant – go on, you can do this!

- Let go of the need for all things to be perfect or exacting

- Recognise that you do not know how to create and share something that is anything but an incredible quality.

reflection prompts

If you've moved through this book in chapter order you will have seen in other chapters that I have shared how one way to gain insight into who you are and to tune into the parts of you to be celebrated – and there are so many of them! – is to do active reflection. These prompts could be used as a theme for journaling, for meditation, for an art practice, or as a discussion topic with a friend or in a collaborative circle with your female friends and sisters. This month, the second in your year of self celebration, continue to create regular time in your schedule for active reflection.

It is such a nourishing and expansive gift for all women to do in ways that honour who you innately are in the world. Each Thrive Factor Archetype has her own ways to reflect. Engaging with the monthly reflection prompts will provide you with insight into how you can use this month's Archetype to support wholistic reflection so as to gain insight and, if it arises, make choices and take action in line with what makes sense and you know is best for you.

The Mediator Diplomat brings reflection to how self balanced and aligned you actually are

She offers you opportunity for inner connection to your truth and the pragmatic, grounded, sensible, value driven way you see the world. The Mediator Diplomat is innately wired to experience and create balance, blend, and alignment, for herself and others. This, like the gifts of the other Thrive Factor Archetypes is something that is often dismissed by women. You are a truth teller, whether you recognise and celebrate that or not. All women have the potential to influence their expression of personal truth and a litmus for justice and equality for all. You do, your friend does, your sister, your colleague, your client, your daughter. Mediator Diplomat women are engaging creators of harmony on a whole other level. The Mediator Diplomat in all of us will be better off for acknowledging this and drawing attention to how to honour your desire to be in your truth. This is to live life fully and totally thriving.

If you know your Thrive Factor Archetypes and know you are a Mediator Diplomat, pay extra attention to these reflection prompts. Use them any time you're feeling the need to create a sense and reality of balance, blend, and alignment in your life. Consider different points of view and know that your strong sense of judgement, right and wrong will serve you well when you keep it in balance with being in your truth and respecting that always. Use them to nurture your value focused soul who always wants to deliver the best experience for all involved, all of the time.

If you don't yet know your Archetypes or are unsure if you are a Mediator Diplomat, you can 100% benefit from these reflections. We each have parts of all 12 Thrive Factor Archetypes within us, so a month of Mediator Diplomat inspired reflections will certainly be exciting and aligning for you.

- **What actions should I take to clearly see what needs to be done in order to achieve the outcome I am working towards?**
- **How can I show myself the same compassion I show others?**
- **As I listen, am I truly hearing what needs to be heard so I can make a fair decision or choice for another or myself?**
- **Is the decision I made fair, equal and balanced? Does it compromise me at all?**
- **Where in my life do I need to mediate for myself and how can I do this with maximum diplomacy?**

- What can I do to acknowledge and celebrate my accomplishments as I continue to strive to meet my high exacting standards?

- What things do I believe in most?

- What can I choose to give a voice to?

- What is my definition of balance and how can I stay reminded of this definition, so it becomes my guiding compass each day?

- What do I love to do that makes me feel great about myself?

- How can I do more of this on a regular basis?

- How can I connect with and trust my intuition?

- What can I do to take care of myself, so I don't experience too much emotional or physical challenge, discomfort or pain?

- How can I feel self justified in all I do and speak?

- What things happen for me that I can see are warning signs that I feel taken advantage of, ignored or mistrusted?

- What boundaries are important for me to put in place to generate balance and harmony?

- What is the line that I am unwilling to cross; the line that will drive me to take confident, clear action to express my boundaries?

- What absolutely annoys me and how can I channel this energy and drive into my business for greater good?

afformations

The Mediator Diplomat's afformations are designed to expand self balance, opening you to trust your truth and to guide you to express it freely so as to be a woman of opinion and contribute your value in the world. Working with afformations creates expansion and a dynamic that opens you to experiencing even more celebration. When you ask the right questions and get playful with discovering answers for them, anything is possible. Afformations are fabulous for journaling, visualisation, or meditation prompts or simply for reflecting.

- **What if I could have fun and be more playful in my days?**
- **What if I only delivered exceptional experiences for all?**
- **What if my personal alignment was easy to create and nurture?**
- **What if my practical and pragmatic ways were also fun?**
- **What if I opened to seeing others truth with respect and gratitude?**
- **What if expressing my truth was welcomed by others?**
- **What if I was already balanced?**
- **What if it was easy to trust who to give my time and energy to?**
- **You could create more afformations of your own to embrace the Mediator Diplomat themes.**

creative exercise

Gorgeous Gratitude Jar with the themes of Self Balance, Self Harmony and Self Alignment

With a strong tendency to perfectionism the Mediator Diplomat can be the first of the Thrive Factor Archetypes to forget to celebrate. Actually, since we are talking about the truth teller here, the truth of the matter is, the Mediator Diplomat can be hugely resistant to celebration. This tends to be driven by the perfectionist within. The awesomely awesome news is that gratitude is an antidote to perfectionism. Her resistance is also contributed to by her sensible, pragmatic approach to life. She can find celebration a bit too much and even comments on it being a waste of time and money. Lucky we each have more than one Archetype.

To bring things back into balance, a regular gratitude practice is such a benefit to any woman. Practicing gratitude supports you to bring a sense of thanks to your world that will ripple out into every part of your life, work, relationships, and sense of self.

Some years ago, I had a client share a variation of this creative exercise. I loved it an immediately began creating my own Glorious Gratitude Jar. I am not a Mediator Diplomat, but I do know the benefit of gratitude and savouring things we are grateful for as a celebration practice. You can be grateful for yourself, for others, for experiences and for things you have.

If gratitude is not something that comes naturally to you, start with practical things like, "I am grateful for fresh water" or "I am grateful it was easier to feel gratitude for something yesterday!" All contributions count. I have no doubt that over the coming month, you'll feel expanded, thankful and open to welcome more gratitude, confidence and magnificence into your life.

your creative exercise invitation

What you need:

- A large clear jar or container with a lid (you don't want your gratitude escaping!)
- Pieces of paper to write on. A small notebook, or notelets work fabulously. Think of sticky note size, but not sticky notes unless you want your gratitude captures to stick together
- Coloured pens
- Anything you want to use to decorate your gratitude captures.

What to do:

- Each day, capture at least one thing you are grateful for by writing it on one of your notes
- Add it to your jar
- Reflect on what you are grateful for, why you are grateful and what role gratitude has in your life
- Smile with enthusiasm and a sense of thanks, as you see the number of things to be grateful for grow in number with each new share.

Thrive Tip: Challenge yourself to add something to your Glorious Gratitude Jar every day this month! And frequently for the months to come. How cool will it be when your jar is overflowing with gratitude.

MEDIATOR DIPLOMAT
SELF-CELEBRATION CHART

this month I...

Did something I wouldn't normally do and had fun	★★★★☆
Spoke my truth, from my heart	★★☆☆☆
Listened to my truth and let it guide me forward	★★★☆☆
Celebrated my value the way others do	★☆☆☆☆
Enjoyed something I would previously have judged	★★★☆☆
Let myself share something that wasn't perfect	★☆☆☆☆
Started a gratitude practice	★★★☆☆
Bought myself a beautiful journal or notebook to capture what I am grateful for	★★★★☆
Understood what it meant to feel balanced and in alignment	★★☆☆☆
Bought myself a gift because I desired it, not because I needed it	★★☆☆☆

Sign up for a year of Bragaudacious self celebration at www.thethrivefactor.com/bragaudacious

self-celebration from around the world

""At least once a week, I will take some time out, go sit at the beach, dig my toes into the sand and just watch the waves roll in and out. This is a special way for me to reflect about my accomplishments over the week and treat myself with some self-kindness and love"

 Rachel Gardiner, Scarborough, WA, Australia

"As a business woman and entrepreneur from the old school generation - we were not taught, told or pushed to celebrate. We didn't talk about how much money we made or the amazing clients we had and certainly not personal wins. It was heads down, bums up and keep working. These days, and I am ecstatic about it, celebrating oneself is something to nurture, enjoy and be celebrated.

Whether it's external - like a client, income, external milestone reached - or internal, celebration is a game changer.   The more one focuses on the joy, gratitude, appreciation, and celebration of life happenings, the more they happen and the happier we are on the way to where we are going.

For myself, I celebrate in a number of ways. For big wins I pop champagne and celebrate the moment with close friends. For little things along the way that bring me joy and light me up, I celebrate with a dance and rampage of appreciation. Even treating myself to some self pleasure like a massage or a crystal or gift is my way of thanking myself and the universe for our co-creative magick"

 Steph Zahalka, Gold Coast, QLD Australia

"How I celebrate now is that I say "thank you" out loud for every payment received. I do an unconscious body wiggle when new clients say 'Yes!" to working with me. I treat myself and my husband to a lovely dinner out when I hit a business goal. And of course - ice cream! Yummy desserts are one way I celebrate and reward a milestone of achievement"

 Serena O'Neil, Perth, WA, Australia

"Smile when you look at yourself in the mirror each morning. You aren't just looking at your eyes, nose, ears, mouth and chin. You are looking at your natural gifts! Nobody can replicate you… absolutely nobody. Your features reflect the remarkable energy and presence you bring to the world. You are one hell of a unique a human being. Celebrating yourself is non-negotiable. Smile, stand up tall, blow yourself a kiss and strut out of that bathroom. And if you trip up on the way out - like I occasionally do… just laugh at yourself and know that's all part of the package"

 Melanie Midegs, Bali, Indonesia

"I am not big on celebrating in the traditional sense. I celebrate by sitting back and witnessing my achievements and acknowledging with gratitude and a bottle of San Peg or Voss sparkling water.

This weekend I celebrated by sitting back with a bottle of San Pelligrino looking over our fully planted veggie garde."

 Eileen Gatsos, Perth, WA, Australia

Month Six
MENTOR TEACHER

archetype themes

**Wisdom, Learning, Guidance,
Transition, Transformation, Knowledge**

goddess inspiration

Hecate

This month we take inspiration from the Mentor Teacher, the sixth of the 12 Thrive Factor Archetypes. She is the Archetype of Wisdom. She's the Wisdom Woman of the Archetypes and curious about what can be learned in the world. A lover of all the lessons available to her, she is an active conduit for information and knowledge. Wise to her very core she can miss the importance of this wisdom in favour for acquiring evidence to demonstrate what she does know, often by her own assessment. As the conduit for knowledge, Mentor Teacher learns something and then shares it. Compulsively. Without thinking. She's considered the font of all things in her friendship and peer circles. Her compulsive desire to share what she has learned is a significant aspect to pay attention to for a Mentor Teacher who pauses and questions her knowledge and expertise can hold back her knowledge and wisdom because she is in a place of mistrust and self judgement. Celebrating the value of all she knows and has experienced is her most treasured lesson.

She can be so determined to prove what she knows she can disconnect from her wisdom, believing all the pieces of paper are needed before she can show up and share. This isn't necessary at all. So many Mentor Teacher women can get so hung up in showing what they know and how much they know that they can dance a fine tuned waltz with owning their wisdom and being arrogant and a show off from a knowledge perspective. When the latter is a reality, there can also be the presence of judgment as the Mentor Teacher decides someone else's value based on her perception of what they know and how they can prove that. Not a fab place to show up and teach from. In fact, it is a threatened Mentor Teacher in the depth of believing she doesn't know enough who's leading from this space.

Nurturing wisdom and understanding it is far more than the learned experience is one of the greatest ways for a Mentor Teacher to show up with value in the world. She is born to share her knowledge and to be a conduit for others seeking to understand. Honouring a life dedicated, often in a compulsive way, to learning all she can, will serve her well. Mindset work to embody the depth of knowledge is warranted to counteract the judgment and criticism of self based on perceived knowledge. You know enough right now. You are the original Wisdom Woman.

I have this Archetype as one of my four cherished Thrive Factor Archetypes. She is the most frequently seen Archetype, alongside the Inspirer Believer in my client and student community. They say like attracts like, and when it comes to a Mentor Teacher woman this couldn't be more truthful. Seeking rich, stimulating conversations, the sharing of opinions and experiences are all things she values. She desires to know what others know and to share what she's spent her lifetime learning. The Mentor Teacher woman was born to teach, to mentor, to guide and she will find herself doing this without question in her work, no matter if she is in a career or self employed. Her teacher traits are often visible early. My favourite game to play as a child was "school", much to the horror of my younger brother who was always the student, expected to fall in line with my strict standards at our school and the harrowing curriculum. In our late 40's he'd tell you that traditional school was ruined for him because of the introduction he received from me. A definite light hearted family moment. Mostly.

The Mentor Teacher, as you learned with all 12 Thrive Factor Archetypes, is present in every woman. She may not actively be part of your Thrive Factor profile, but she exists within you in some way. She is the part of you who is curious and inquisitive about the world. She is the part of you who loves throwing yourself into courses, programs, workshops, books, podcasts, and masterclasses. She is the part of you who can make sense of seemingly complex concepts and translate them into pieces of information that are easier for others to engage with and learn.

She is also the part of you who can question herself and wonder if she really does know anything at all. She is the part of you who over thinks, judges yourself and others based on a measure of knowledge. She is the part of you who wastes so much time thinking you need to know more in order to be able to share what you know as a teacher, a mentor or a guide. She is the part of you who denies what she has learned and makes incorrect assumptions that everyone else knows what she does. She is the part of you who exchanges intellectual accomplishments with credibility, shying away from your lived experience and life lessons as having the value to truly do.

She is the part of you who finds yourself wanting the to learn all she can about all the things. Draw on her depth of wisdom, her intuitive insights, her ability to translate knowledge and information for others to understand with greater ease. Immerse yourself in opportunities where your curiosity and natural inquisitive nature get to expand and engage with the world. Engage with her gift for sharing and trusting what she knows, knowing it has value and is so wildly needed.

the mentor teachers greatest gift to give herself is self learning

What is self learning?

- It is being aware of what you already know
- It is recognising your life lessons are as valuable as the ones you have learned in more formal learning environments
- It is acknowledging the value of your wisdom
- It is knowing that you don't know everything, but you certainly do know more than many other people
- It is engaging actively with all the available learning
- It is taking action on what you learn and implementing things into your life and work
- It is being open and curious about what is out there in the world for you.

mentor teacher and self celebration

With your love of learning and the generous volume of time you spend adding to your knowledge and expertise your Mentor Teacher within can be resistant to self celebration, seeing is as lacking in value when compared to all the learning and sharing you do.

This month, to honour the parts of you that are

Insightful, Intuitive, Wise, Guiding, Trusting,
Ingenious and Knowledgeable

This is your invitation to spend time tuning into your inner wisdom in ways that feel like you're truly showing up and showing yourself how much you trust what you know

Understanding how to be a Wisdom Woman for herself is something your inner Mentor Teacher will love to immerse herself in learning. It's not always the easiest thing for a Mentor Teacher to do, to open to her wisdom and recognise its depth, breadth and value. It is possibly not the easiest thing for you to do either, whether you are a Mentor Teacher or not.

- You find yourself falling into overthinking as a default
- You find yourself mistrusting what you know, believing another piece of paper or qualification that proves your learning is needed to move forward – it isn't
- You find yourself unsure of how to share your wisdom, because you think you need to learn or know more
- You find yourself wondering if your lived and learning experience is really that valuable after all
- You find yourself falling into a pattern of learning more in place of trusting yourself, your intuition, and your clear, tangible insights.

You find yourself saying (often only to yourself for fear of being considered silly or not knowledgeable enough) "I just want to share what I know" even though the words you hear come from your inner drive are saying "you know so much already" or "what you know is so valuable and appreciated" or "you are here to guide others to connect with their own wisdom and purpose."

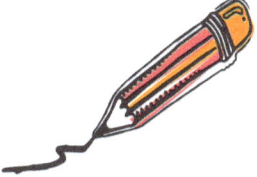

to celebrate yourself is to

- Show gratitude to yourself for all you have immersed yourself in from a learning perspective
- Show gratitude to your favourite teachers and mentors
- Connect with other wise women and start wisdom infused conversations that get you thinking and inspire you in some way
- Increase the prices of your courses or programs if you are a business woman!
- Reflect on all the courses you have taken and the tangible things you have learned about yourself, or that you can and have applied to your career or business
- Embody how good it feels when someone thanks you for helping them with something
- Invest in a learning experience for fun, not necessarily to acquire new knowledge
- Buy a new book you have been coveting for some time
- Trust your intuition, knowing it is always working in your favour and the good of all
- Listen to the messages you receive from within
- Turn what you know into something you can freely share with others
- Recognise how much others value what you know and what you have learned.

reflection prompts

If you've moved through this book in chapter order you will have seen in other chapters that I have shared how one key way to gain insight into who you are and to tune into the parts of you to be celebrated – and there are so many of them! – is to do active reflection. These prompts could be used as a theme for journaling, for meditation, for an art practice, or as a discussion topic with a friend. This month, the potential sixth in your year of self celebration continue to create regular time in your schedule for active reflection. It is such a nourishing and expansive gift for all women to do in ways that honour who you innately are in the world. Each Thrive Factor Archetype has her own ways to reflect. Engaging with the monthly reflection prompts will provide you with insight into how you can use this month's Archetype to support wholistic reflection so as to gain insight and, if it arises, make choices and take action in line with what makes sense and you know is best for you.

The Mentor Teacher brings reflection to how self learned, wisdom fuelled and trusting in your knowledge you actually are

She offers you opportunity for inner connection to your sense of wisdom, desire for knowledge, ability to quickly grasp and make sense of concepts and also to your desire to be the ultimate Wisdom Woman for others. The Mentor Teacher is innately wired to experience and create a transmission of knowledge across the world, for the benefit of herself and all people. This, like the gifts of the other Thrive Factor Archetypes is something that is often dismissed by women. You are a true conduit of knowledge, whether you recognise and celebrate that fact or not. All women have the potential to influence with knowledge – the combination of your valuable lived and learned experience. You do, your friend does, your sister, your colleague, your client, your daughter. Mentor Teacher women are teachers, guides, and mentors on a whole other level to women who are not Mentor Teachers. The true Wisdom Women of the world. The Mentor Teacher in all of us will be better off for acknowledging this and drawing attention to how to honour your desire to be wise and trust in that incredible wisdom you can tap into at any time for you and for others. This is so as to live life fully and totally thriving.

If you know your Thrive Factor Archetypes and know you are a Mentor Teacher, pay extra attention to these reflection prompts. Use them any time you're feeling the need to break free, to break things before you break down, to define solutions, when you're into analytical mode and overanalysing and over engineering everything, when you crave ease and effortlessness. Use them when you're craving space and freedom. Use them to nurture your liberation fuelled heart that believes every soul deserves to know what it is to be free of whatever real and perceived limits, blocks, restrictions and patterns hold them back. If you don't yet know your Archetypes or are unsure if you are a Mentor Teacher you can 100% benefit from these reflections. We each have parts of all 12 Thrive Factor Archetypes within us, so a month of Mentor Teacher inspired reflections will certainly be exciting and freeing for you.

- What lesson am I trying to convey in this situation?
- What do I most need to learn for my business/career/work? For myself?
- How can I freely share my knowledge without giving away my intellectual property?
- How can I freely share my knowledge without undercharging or missing out from profiting from my wisdom?
- What lessons can I teach to inspire my students, clients or community and encourage them to be excited to search for the answers themselves?
- What have been the greatest lessons I have learned and that I come back to again and again?
- How can I continue to use these lessons in my career/business and in my life?

- What do I value most about my knowledge, experience, and expertise? And how am I using this in my career/business?
- Where do I find myself teaching or mentoring and what do my clients, students, community need most?
- How can I share the right amount of information without feeling fearful about what I am sharing?
- How can I stay 'in the moment', attentive and focused on the task at hand?
- What is it about teaching that I love and how can I inject that into all of my interactions with real and potential students, clients, community?
- Why is it so important for me to learn new things and to share my learning with others?
- How do I implement, trust and work with the knowledge and experiences I already have, instead of looking to gather more information?
- What is the right amount of information for me to share to assist others without overwhelming them?
- How can I expand how much I trust and value what I already know?
- What does wisdom mean to me?
- What do I love to share and why?

afformations

The Mentor Teacher's afformations are designed to expand self wisdom, opening you to trust your wisdom, your lived and learned experience and collected knowledge and to guide you to teach, guide, mentor, and support from the place of your wisdom and ingeniousness – personally and professionally. Working with afformations creates expansion and a dynamic that opens you to experiencing even more celebration. When you ask the right questions and get playful with discovering answers for them, anything is possible. Afformations are fabulous for journaling, visualisation, or meditation prompts or simply for reflecting.

- What if sharing my wisdom was a path to greater joy in my life?
- What if the knowledge I already have was valued more than I realised by others?
- What if I could tap into my lived and learned experience to guide others to achieve the life, career, business, relationship (or whatever else they desire) that they wish to have as reality?
- What if I valued my wisdom and knowledge as much as others do?
- What if I could trust what I already know?
- What if I could effortlessly find the answers, I seek without enrolling in a load of new courses that I probably won't finish?
- What if I did know the answer/s when others asked me question/s?
- What if my ingeniousness (the expression of my lived and learned experience) was my superpower?
- You could create more afformations of your own to embrace the Mentor Teacher themes.

creative exercise

Wisdom Collection with the themes of
Self Learning, Self Trust and Self Knowledge

One of the greatest ways to connect with and often to remember how wise we are is to actually create a collection of our wisdom experience across a period of time. The invitation to you for the Mentor Teacher month is to do just that. To create a Wisdom Collection for the month. You may decide you love this so much that you continue it for the rest of the year or for a whole 365 days.

How do you do this? With as much simplicity as possible.

The Mentor Teacher can be very good at overthinking things, much like the Mediator Diplomat. It's much like the good student at school trying to get an A+ for her submission. Let that go and be in your wisdom zone. Trust your inner guidance and intuition and celebrating the clarity and insights afforded you while you actively focus on creating your Wisdom Collection. Use what you have learned about the Mentor Teacher across this month to be a guide as you learn more about the wisdom you already have access to.

What counts as wisdom?

Anything you wish it to be. It could be an aha moment, an inspiring quote that got you thinking. Maybe it was something you said to someone else. Or it could be something you wrote in your journal or a thought you had. It all counts. Anything can be wisdom!

your creative exercise invitation

There are a handful of easy to follow steps to create your Wisdom Collection.

What you need:

- A container to save all of your wisdom insights. This could be a gift box, a jar, or something that feels special and where you are going to enjoy saving all you connect with this month, or year
- Paper to write on. Perhaps you have a notebook where you could tear out the pages, or a stack of small notelets you can easily write on. I love to have one of the square note taking stack on hand, the kind you can get at most stationers
- Pens! Coloured pens, a single favourite colour, a silver one or gold pen even. Whatever feels in keeping with the depth of your wisdom and excitement about reconnecting with it
- A dedicated time in the day to reflect on your key wisdom for the day. I call this my Yoda time. Some years ago, a small group of my business coaching clients in a program with me at the time started calling me Business (or Biz) Yoda. Aside from the fact Yoda is my all-time favourite Star Wars character, my first name, Shannon, has its origins in Ireland and means 'little old wise one'! So I totally owned it and still get referred to as Yoda on a regular basis. This reminds me instantly of my wisdom and how valued it is by others in the world. Yay for that!

What to do:

- In your dedicated wisdom reflection time, consider what you have heard, said or shared during the day and capture on your note paper, a key take away or insight – the wise words you hear from you
- Place the date on your wisdom insight
- Put your wisdom insight note into your box
- Keep doing this daily across the month, or extend it out throughtout the year
- Any time you doubt your wisdom, or need a boost to reconnect with this incredible power you have then go into your Wisdom Collection and take out one of your wisdom insights. Read it and take it on board for whatever is happening at the time, or on the day you read it! I am sure it'll be valuable, and it is also an incredible way to celebrate how wise you are
- At the end of the time, you keep your Wisdom Collection, create time and space to read over everything you have collected. Over time your notes will likely have ended up out of date order. That is ideal. Wisdom has no timeline, so read them as they come to you and honour what you know, who you are and how you share all this magic and wisdom in the world.

Thrive Tip: As you take one of your wisdom insights out during the month, use it as a reflection for a visualisation, mediation or as a journal prompt to deepen your connection to this one piece of wisdom!

MENTOR TEACHER
SELF-CELEBRATION CHART

this month I...

Completed a course I started some time ago and acknowledged my accomplishment	★★★★☆
Recognised all I know already and shared something to support another's learning	★★☆☆☆
Re-read my favourite book	★★★☆☆
Trusted myself when asked a question about something I know and answered from trust	★☆☆☆☆
Listened to a wisdom infused masterclass, podcast or workshop	★★★☆☆
Acted on what I learned and implemented right away	★☆☆☆☆
Reflected on all the things I have learned in the past year and felt proud	★★★☆☆
Gifted a book I have loved to someone I think will enjoy reading it	★★★★☆
Owned my inner Wisdom Woman for the gift she has been throughout my life	★★☆☆☆
Acknowledged how valuable my knowledge and wisdom have been	★★☆☆☆

Sign up for a year of Bragaudacious self celebration at www.thethrivefactor.com/bragaudacious

self-celebration from around the world

"I love celebrating every milestone no matter big or small. I think it's important to not forget to celebrate ourselves because we often overlook how great and valuable, we are. My favourite way to celebrate is taking time off and spend it outdoor alone because that's my happy place and where I experience genuine joy"

 Penny Soo, Auckland, New Zealand

"Why was my mind unusually blank when asked the question, "how do I celebrate myself as a woman?"

Maybe it's a misinterpretation of the word and what we have traditionally come to expect of a celebration. Festivities, fanfare, family, friends, food and the accompanying pops of champagne!

But, my celebration of self is far less assuming and wanting of fanfare. It is quiet. It is an inner feeling that flows into my equally quiet confidence of self. But hey, that said, sometimes a pop of champagne is a very welcomed accompaniment"

 Donna Fortune, Perth, Western Australia, Australia

"I celebrate every day because I create miracles every single day. I live in a constant state of celebration. Every day in my life is unique, special, and somewhat magical. When I am going through a hard time, I celebrate the love and support of my people, the lessons I am in the process of learning, as well as the knowing that the moon has to be fully dark in order to shine. When I have huge wins, I celebrate by anchoring the feelings of gratitude, pride, and satisfaction it brings"

 Em Ducharme, Montreal, Canada

"Celebration...the word itself leads us to celebrate the "good" things that happen in our lives. What if...just for a moment, we flipped the script?

What if we started to celebrate the things that we perceive as "bad"? I know it is a stretch, bear with me.

We know some of our greatest blessings come from our greatest lessons. So, if we started celebrating those lessons, almost in advance, knowing that a blessing is coming, imagine how amazing it could be.

If we got excited about "failure", if we celebrated one less way that we have to try to make it work, if we celebrated our challenges as hard as our wins, pretty soon we would just celebrate everything.

I don't know about you, but I LOVE to feel the rush of celebrations. The one thing that I do know above all, is this, the more you celebrate, no matter how big, small, good or bad, the more you will have to celebrate! I think that, is one way that we can start to change the world"

 Julie Paulston, Pensacola, Florida USA

Month Seven
MOTHER NURTURER

archetype themes

Caring, Mothering, Empowerment, Guidance, Nurturing, Self Care, Self Love

goddess inspiration

Demeter and Gaia

This month we take inspiration from the Mother Nurturer, the seventh of the 12 Thrive Factor Archetypes. She is the Archetype of Nurture. She's best described as being like a huge, warm, often overbearing hug. Taking care of others, with a focus on taking care of all those she considers family, is her main agenda in life.

A traditional woman here to uphold traditional family values, the Mother Nurturer is a woman who strongly desires to have children, no matter how that happens. Not all Mother Nurturers do get to bare their own children, but they will still find a way to care for children, families, and the things they birth or bring to life. It isn't uncommon for a Mother Nurturer to birth a business for example.

She can be so focused on taking care of everyone else, that self care and self nurture are at the bottom of the list of priorities for a Mother Nurturer. She wishes to be surrounded with those she loves and adores entertaining family and friends. Food and particularly sharing a nourishing meal, is a way she sees she can show her love for those she most cares about. It's not about fancy food – it is always about good, old fashioned, nourishing food that fills bellies and hearts at the same time. When I think of this kind of Mother Nurturer care, I think of Nana's apple pie with a big scoop of ice cream.

Taking care of herself is not the first thought for a Mother Nurturer. It is always about others and their needs. This can leave Mother Nurturer feeling depleted and questioning if all the love she shares so generously is even appreciated. It is important for Mother Nurturer to show herself the appreciation she wishes to receive from external sources, so that she fills her own tank first. Just like an oxygen mask in an aeroplane, fit your own mask first so you can help others in need. A Mother Nurturer who's running on empty, or heading that way, can become needy and have her greatest fear turn from a thought into reality. Mother Nurturers greatest fear is that she is not wanted and appreciated by those she loves the most, starting with her family. Her dread of this fear becoming real can also trigger a martyr complex that is never going to warm her to others. In fact it can quickly repel.

The Mother Nurturer, as you learned with previous Archetypes is, like all 12 Thrive Factor Archetypes, present in every woman. She may not actively be part of your Thrive Factor profile, but she exists within you in some way. She is the part of you who loves to take care of others. She is the part of you who wants to empower others and learns that leading by example is the greatest form of empowerment. She is the part of you who is generous, giving and kind. She is the part of you who others call on for support, knowing you'll be there in their time of need. She is also the part of you who gives too much and drains herself. She is the part of you who places self care way down the list, even when you intellectually know it is important. She is the part of you who says yes first and then can get grumpy when you haven't left any time to do what you wanted to do for you. She is the part of you who so desperately wants to be included by your family that you can push them away when you shift from mothering to smothering.

She is the part of you who loves being a part of the family, particularly when you take on the matriarch role. Draw on her generosity, her big heart, her abundant ability to love and care for one and all. Take her kindness and her ability to make others feel loved and included as reminders you too have these qualities. Embrace all the qualities shared with the outside world and turn them inwards to yourself so you feel as loved, nurtured, cared for and loved as others feel in your presence. Give to yourself first, knowing that you are going to be the very best version of yourself for everyone – your real and perceived family – is going to bring you joy filled satisfaction and a sense of accomplishment and purpose in life, for your entire life. You deserve to feel cared for and needed as much as you make others feel loved and appreciated.

the mother nurturer's greatest gift to give herself is self nurture

What is self nurture?

- It is recognising when you need to take care of yourself so you can take care of others the way you desire to
- It is doing things that make you feel loved and cared for
- It is realising that taking care of you as a priority means you are a the best version of you for those most important in your life, your family
- It is being gentle and kind to yourself
- It is filling up your love tank so there is always an abundance of love and care to go around (the Mother Nurturer creative exercise will help with this!)
- It is eating nourishing food that makes you feel fabulous and energised from the inside out
- It is being able to say yes to you and know that it doesn't mean you are saying no to others.

mother nurturer and self celebration

With your big heart and genuine desire to take care of everyone and anyone you vaguely consider family, often to the detriment of your self care, every Mother Nurturer within can be resistant to self celebration, particularly as it's seen, through a Mother Nurturers lens as unnecessary, unless it's leading the celebration of a family member.

This month, to honour the parts of you that are

Generous, Loving, Kind, Inclusive, Nurturing
Supportive and Big Hearted

This is your invitation to spend time truly nurturing yourself in ways that feel like you're giving yourself what you so freely give to others you care about!

Being a cheerleader for self care and self nurture is something your inner Mother Nurturer will be benefit from understanding and embodying. It's not always the easiest thing for a Mother Nurturer to do. It is possibly not the easiest thing for you to do either, whether you are a Mother Nurturer or not.

- You find yourself putting everyone else before yourself
- You find yourself abandoning self care in the event that someone you love might need you
- You find yourself ignoring your own needs because it's uncomfortable to give to yourself first
- You find yourself wanting to feel loved and appreciated and deciding you're not really valued
- You find yourself falling into martyrdom, believing you are the only one capable of providing the love, care and support your real and perceived family need

You find yourself saying (often only to yourself for fear of being proved you are unlovable) "I just want my family together and for everyone to get along with each other" even though the words you hear come from your heart are saying "you have given them exactly what they need, now let them find their wings and fly" or "you are loved and appreciated" or "you are doing an incredible job supporting everyone!"

to celebrate yourself is to

- Recognise how valued you are by those in your life who matter the most
- Blend self care with how much you care for other people
- Show yourself all the love and appreciation you desire to receive from others
- Head to the day spa and indulge in luxurious treatments that make you feel nourished and pampered
- Sleep in and order breakfast in bed from your family
- Buy yourself a gift that fills your heart with joy and love
- Speak to yourself with the same support and love you show to all those you care about
- Practice regular gratitude with an open heart and all the kindness you so generously share
- Nourish your thoughts, your body, your emotions, your soul, anyway that feels energising and loving
- Book a babysitter for the children and go out with your partner, friends or someone you have fun with
- Keep a commitment you made for you, even when – particularly when – a family member wants your help – you'll never see that someone else could help, or that your family member will work out a solution if you always drop everything and show up for them
- Turn off your phone, shut the kids out and sit with a cuppa and a fabulous book, even for 5 minutes a day – precious mum/caregiver time.

reflection prompts

If you have flowed this book in chapter order you will have seen in other chapters that I have shared that one way to gain insight into who you are and to tune into the parts of you to be celebrated – and there are so many of them! – is to do active reflection. These prompts could be used as a theme for journaling, for meditation, for an art practice, or as a discussion topic with a friend. This month, the second in your year of self celebration, continue to create regular time in your schedule for active reflection.

It is such a nourishing and expansive gift for all women to do in ways that honour who you innately are in the world. Each Thrive Factor Archetype has her own ways to reflect. Engaging with the monthly reflection prompts will provide you with insight into how you can use this month's Archetype to support wholistic reflection so as to gain insight and, if it arises, make choices and take action in line with what makes sense and you know is best for you.

The Mother Nurturer brings reflection to how self nurturing and in a place of self appreciation you are

She offers you opportunity for to connect to your generosity and give to yourself as abundantly as you give to others when it comes to caring and nurturing, supporting and guiding. The Mother Nurturer is innately wired to care for and nurture others, and mostly before she'd ever consider doing this for herself. This, like the gifts of the other Thrive Factor Archetypes is something that is often dismissed by women. Not perhaps as much as some of the other archetypal gifts, because so many of us live in cultures where women are predominantly the care givers in their families and communities. You are a big hearted, nurturing soul, whether you recognise and celebrate that fact or not. All women have the potential to care in abundance. You do, your friend does, your sister, your colleague, your client, your daughter. Mother Nurturer women are overwhelmingly gifted with the tendency to smother the world with love and support.

The Mother Nurturer in all of us will be better off for acknowledging this and drawing attention to how to honour your desire to care for others while prioritising caring for and nurturing yourself so you can be the best you for those you love the most. This is so as to live life fully and totally thriving. If you know your Thrive Factor Archetypes and know you are a Mother Nurturer, pay extra attention to these reflection prompts. Use them any time you're feeling the need for self care, or feeling overwhelmed by the demands of taking care of your real and perceived family. Use them when you're craving love and appreciation and feeling like you are not as valued as you wish to be. Use them to nurture your big, loving heart that believes every person in the world deserves to know what it is to belong and be a part of a family.

If you don't yet know your Archetypes or are unsure if you are a Mother Nurturer you can 100% benefit from these reflections. We each have parts of all 12 Thrive Factor Archetypes within us, so a month of Mother Nurturer inspired reflections will certainly be exciting and freeing for you.

- **How can I mother and nurture my children in a way that empowers them?**
- **What can I do for myself to fulfill my own needs?**
- **What needs do I actually have?**
- **How can I take care of myself and be the independent woman I know I can be?**
- **What ways can I give my love and yet maintain a healthy distance so as not to smother others?**
- **What is my definition of self-care?**

- What self-care activities do I really enjoy?
- How can I give these to myself on a regular basis, knowing they will support me in my mothering role?
- How can I be empowering and encouraging for my family?
- What need am I trying to fulfill when I feel the urge to interfere in my children's, grandchildren's and family's lives?
- How can I let my family and loved ones be free to be themselves and guide them rather than smother them?
- What sort of a life do I want for myself and how can I go out and live it without relying upon or allowing myself to be distracted by the perceived and real needs of my family?
- How do I define freedom and what can I do to create freedom for myself?
- When did I last do something just for me and why is taking care of myself such a sporadic experience?
- How can I focus on the love and acknowledgment all around me and remember that I have everything I need; and that I can give myself what I feel is most important first and foremost?
- What triggers my 'mother guilt' and how can I counteract these triggers?

afformations

The Mother Nurturer's afformations are designed to expand self nurturing, opening you to trust your big heart and its desire to care for others, turning that love for the world into yourself so you benefit across all aspects of your life, personally and professionally. Working with afformations creates expansion and a dynamic that opens you to experiencing even more celebration. When you ask the right questions and get playful with discovering answers for them, anything is possible. Afformations are fabulous for journaling, visualisation or meditation prompts or simply for reflecting.

- What if I could give myself all the love and care I so freely give to others?
- What if I was appreciated and valued and didn't need to seek that externally?
- What if I trusted my loved ones had all they needed from me to live rich, fulfilled lives?
- What if I nurtured myself first?
- What if my big heart was the source of the nurturing I crave?
- What if my mothering instincts were available to guide my life, as well as the lives of my family and loved ones?
- What if my relationship with myself was a priority?
- What if I had access to all the love, kindness and nurturing I desire, any time I wish for it?
- You could create more afformations of your own to embrace the Mother Nurturer themes.

creative exercise

Self Love Tank with the themes of
Self Nurture, Self Love and Self Appreciation

I remember creating this creative exercise well over a decade ago when I led self awareness and creative expansion workshops and programs for women. Calling on my Transpersonal Art Therapy and counselling background and my lifelong love of personal development, I led a program called Creative Goddess. It was a 6 week experience where each week we met a group of 3 goddesses and completed an inspired creative exercise together. The week we focused on mother goddesses this was the creative exercise; to create a self love tank.

The intention behind this creative fun experience was to recognise that you would rarely feel depleted and fall into the space of martyrdom so common for a Mother Nurturer, when you were able to give to yourself before you gave to others. It's a well known fact that many women who are actually mothers or care givers can struggle to give to themselves. So they approach and exist in the world with a self love tank that's very low or near empty all the time.

your creative exercise invitation

In introducing this exercise, I always used the analogy of preparing for a long journey in the car. One of the first things any person driving would do is ensure there is enough petrol, or gas in the tank. You'd know how long it took to get to your destination and prepare accordingly to successfully arrive where you were headed. For you to get to your desired end point safely your vehicle needs to have plenty of resources in the fuel tank and the ability to refuel if the journey is a longer distance. Life is a long journey. Regular stops to refuel means the journey you experience as life is that much more enjoyable, and likely fun to share with others.

What you need:

- Sheets of coloured paper in colours that feel nourishing and energising to you. I found pinks, reds, purples and colours associated with the heart were popular, but choose what you love most. If you don't have access to coloured paper you could use white and colour in the paper in your favourite, nourishing colours
- A marker pen to write with
- A template of a heart that you can trace around – something the width of a standard coffee cup or glass worked well
- A large sheet of blank card, A3 size minimum. The bigger, the better and the colour doesn't matter
- Glue stick
- Scissors
- A place to hang your Self Love Tank.

What to do:

1. Trace a bunch of hearts onto your coloured paper
2. Cut the hearts out and place them in a bowl or container so you can access them easily
3. Draw a large heart on your large sheet of blank card
4. At least once a day write something on one of your hearts – something heart-warming that happened in your day, a kind word you received, something you did for yourself, anything that felt nurturing
5. Glue to heart onto the bigger heart – your Self Love Tank
6. Over the month watch your Self Love Tank fill up as a beautiful reminder of all the love available to you at any time.

Thrive Tip: If you have children or grandchildren tell them what you are creating and ask them to remind you to fill your Self Love Tank at least once a day! They will have some awesome suggestions and contributions for you, adding to the love and support you feel. That right there, is a top up to your Self Love Tank.

MOTHER NURTURER
SELF-CELEBRATION CHART

this month I...

Created a Self Love Tank! (see this month's Creative Exercise for inspiration)	★★★★☆
Added to my Self Love Tank each day	★★☆☆☆
Invested in something that felt nourishing and loving just for me	★★★☆☆
Showed myself the kindness I always show others	★☆☆☆☆
Spoke to myself with a loving tone	★★★☆☆
Kept a gratitude journal to remind myself just how much there is to be thankful for	★☆☆☆☆
Let my family do something that showed they cared	★★★☆☆
Put myself first, even though my instinct was to drop my plans and help others	★★★★☆
Enjoyed enriching food that felt wonderful and abundant to eat	★★☆☆☆
Appreciated myself for who I am and all I do	★★☆☆☆

Sign up for a year of Bragaudacious self celebration at www.thethrivefactor.com/bragaudacious

self-celebration from around the world

"How do I celebrate as a woman 'I stay true to myself and follow my passion, even when it might go against what everyone else thinks I should be doing.' Oh and I didn't think to share this for Bragaudacious but you can include it if you want – I am taking a moment to say 'f_ck yeah' to this I've only started celebrating in the last year as I was always chasing my next goal and not stopping to celebrate the wins"

 Natalie Briney, Margaret River, WA, Australia

"No matter how big or small your win – you have to celebrate every step, move and thought you co-create in the life that you are living. Life is for living, and when we as thriving ladies of the world acknowledge the wins of life, everything just flows"

 Sam Evans, London, UK

"I celebrate through experiencing all the senses - taste, tough, sight, smell, and sound - anything that reconnects me to unconditional love and the natural elements!"

 Lauren Quelhurst, Baldivis, WA, Australia

"Celebration to me has grown and evolved immensely over the years, and I'm excited and grateful to be share my thoughts and ways that I embrace celebration here. This has been a source of deep growth for me in recent moments, so I was incredibly honored when Shannon asked me to write some words about how I celebrate. *[Author note: I am so happy you were honoured Lyndsay, Shannon x]*

For the longest time celebration was something I did externally. In the heat of excitement, I would do something big, loud and bold. My favorite for the longest time was to buy plane tickets on a whim and take myself on a trip, or to buy a stunning new dress to feel amazing and to show myself off. As I've been exploring this topic more recently though my celebrations have shifted. I recognized that by doing things, like buying big trips or material items for myself it was so I could show off. To show others how amazing I am. I used it as a way to fill a void only I could fill. Celebration to me was then used as a tool to make me feel important and good enough. Now, I still love to buy myself wonderful things and incredible experiences however the ways I do them and they way I celebrate is vastly different.

I celebrate internally. To me, celebration is a feeling. Like butterflies in the stomach. I give myself ample space to really go within. Perhaps I'll have a lovely drink or take myself out to a nice dinner, often with my journal. I sit and slowly embrace myself. I reflect and honor the woman I was before the thing I'm celebrating. I honor the woman I was during the evolution…. the challenges, struggles and overcoming's within me. I honor the woman I've become. My form of celebration is a deeply internal, intimate experience. It's important to me to fully give thanks to every version of myself along the way. To see her, to appreciate her, to thank her. It's important to me to truly love every moment of the adventure and to reflect upon the perfection of how everything was and is. To me, this is the greatest way to honor the journey and the path. To celebrate ones Self. To celebrate the path, the courage, the depth, the bravery, the dreamer and the doer. Only after I do this, do I intentionally decide and ask the woman I am now how she would like to celebrate. It may well be a trip, a new outfit, or pair of shoes. It may also be an intimate night in. Either way, it's the internal celebration and revelry that's become most important to me"

 Lindsay Dam, Hood River, Oregon, USA

Month Eight
NETWORKER CONNECTOR

archetype themes

Connection, Self Connection, Socialising, Community, Value

goddess inspiration

Ixchel

This month we take inspiration from the Networker Connector, the eight of the 12 Thrive Factor Archetypes. She is the Archetype of connection. She's always up for a party or event and relishes in the notion and reality of meeting anyone – someone known to her and all the new people in the world.

A woman on a mission to surround herself with the best people she can find, the Networker Connector can spend so much time out and about that time on her own is little to non-existent. Being in her own company can be intensely uncomfortably for her, but so necessary. Learning to be in this discomfort and asking for support to shift it is a true gift any Networker Connector will benefit from giving to herself. Self connection is essential for any Networker Connector woman. This is not something she gives to herself with the same vigour she applies to creating magical introductions in the world. Often the Networker Connector finds time alone to be one of the most pointless activities. When this shifts and she is able to celebrate the alone time as precious in her busy schedule, the quality and value of all connections she makes – with self and others – amplifies significantly.

She can be so determined to connect others that her self care and balance between work and play can easily swing in the favour of no self care. There's a party happening somewhere after all. When on a mission to bring the world together she is a force to be behold, but when she approaches this mission with an empty tank the outcome will be disappointing and something she judges herself for unfairly. As a quick side note, a Liberator Engineer woman can sometimes be confused for being a Networker

Connector. She's not. A Liberator Engineer is about connecting the pieces of the big vision puzzle she sees – for her it is about connecting things that include people. For a Networker Connector it is always about people first. She's often an extrovert when she's purely in her Networker Connector energy and I am grateful on behalf of every Networker Connector that she has a set of other Archetypes to balance this energy and make self connection more effortless, even if it comes from burnout and necessity, instead of by choice which is the ultimate expression taking into account self celebration.

The Networker Connector, as you learned with all 12 Thrive Factor Archetypes, is present in every woman. She may not actively be part of your Thrive Factor profile, but she exists within you in some way. She is the part of you who enjoys the company of people, on your terms. She is the part of you who loves to get ready for a party or event. She is the part of you who gets a buzz out of meeting people and knowing exactly the ideal person or people to introduce that individual to for magic to happen because of the connection made. She is also the part of you who can easily over indulge and find yourself saying yes to too many things and invitations.

She is the part of you who then feels over stretched and uncertain how to come back you yourself to fill up your depleted reserves. She is the part of you who doesn't understand the power of no. She is the part of you who finds yourself wanting to be seen and appreciated for the connection you share freely and generously in the world. Draw on her desire to create genuine connection. Understand the immense value of time alone and respect yourself enough to welcome reciprocation when it comes to benefiting from your network. A self connected Networker Connector is a valued woman on an expanded, much loved scale.

the networker connector's greatest gift to give herself is self connection

What is self connection?

- It is benefiting from the extensive community of people you have invested time and energy to build and nurture
- It is spending time alone on a regular basis to recharge, even if you are a naturally extroverted person who is energised by time with other people
- It is seeing the value inherent in the relationships you have created
- It is doing things that connect you to your intuition and sense of self
- It is scheduling quiet time to balance out the busyness of being so active in the world, socialising and burning the candle at both ends day after day and night after night
- It is learning to be comfortable and recognise the value of time with yourself
- It is journaling, mediating, visualising and reflecting on who you are and the wild, beautiful value you have within.

networker connector and self celebration

With your love of being with people, making generous connections, often to the detriment of your personal wellbeing, every Networker Connector within can be resistant to self celebration. This Archetype loves a good party, but things for herself do not always come naturally.

This month, to honour the parts of you that are

Social, Extroverted, Inclusive, A people lover, Energised,
Willing and Always generous with your introductions

This is your invitation to spend time taking care of yourself in ways that feel like you're truly caring for you!

Being able to see the value inherent within the network she has created for herself is something your inner Networker Connector will benefit from learning and actioning. It's not always the easiest thing for a Networker Connector to do. It is possibly not the easiest thing for you to do either, whether you are a Networker Connector or not.

- You find yourself focusing on who you know and who you can connect
- You find yourself feeling awkward benefiting from your network and shying away from asking for the same kind of help and support others so effortlessly ask of you
- You find yourself burning every candle you own at all their ends and burning yourself out instead of taking time to rest – there's no FOMO for you because you're there at every invitation!
- You find yourself uncertain as to how to balance the energy of the Networker Connector with the reality she is only one aspect of you
- You find yourself resisting time on your own, because a party for one isn't that fun.

You find yourself saying (often only to yourself for fear of being considered self focused or not valuable to others) "I just want to feel valued and connected" even though the words you hear come from your inner drive are saying "say yes to the invitation because imagine who could be there" or "you don't need to spend time at home, the world is waiting for you" or "they won't really help, you got this all on your own!"

to celebrate yourself is to

- Understand you are valued for who you are, not who you know
- Learn the true, infinite value of the network and community you have built and nurtured
- Ask for what you want, need and desire
- Open to trusting when you ask for support it will be provided – others are as generous and grateful for your support as you are for theirs so when you ask, your generosity will be reciprocated
- Start your day with self connection before racing out into the world
- Say no when you don't want to go to an event
- Spend time with those who nourish you
- Release your independence that comes from thinking no one will be there for you like you are for them and seek out guidance to connect with yourself more effortlessly
- Increase the prices of all your services if you are in business knowing they offer so much value others recognise and will pay for happily
- Add down time to your schedule daily
- Sit in the discomfort that can arise from being in your own company and resist being with others all the time
- Enjoy time alone, particularly when your instincts and desire are saying you should really be at some event.

reflection prompts

If you've progressed through Bragaudacious in chapter order you will have seen in other chapters I have shared how one way to gain insight into who you are and to tune into the parts of you to be celebrated – and there are so many of them! – is to do active reflection. These prompts could be used as a theme for journaling, for meditation, for an art practice, or as a discussion topic with a friend. This month, the second in your year of self celebration, continue to create regular time in your schedule for active reflection.

It is such a nourishing and expansive gift for all women to do in ways that honour who you innately are in the world. Each Thrive Factor Archetype has her own ways to reflect. Engaging with the monthly reflection prompts will provide you with insight into how you can use this month's Archetype to support wholistic reflection so as to gain insight and, if it arises, make choices and take action in line with what makes sense and you know is best for you.

The Networker Connector brings reflection to how self connected and self valuing you truly are

She offers you opportunity for inner connection to truth of your value and importance in the world, to be open to see the depth of how appreciated you are by all who know you. The Networker Connector is innately wired to experience and create connection between others in the world, but the richness of that connection comes down to how connected she is to herself. This, like the gifts of the other Thrive Factor Archetypes is something that is often dismissed by women. You are a true weaver of people, creating magic with every introduction you facilitate, whether you recognise and celebrate that fact or not. All women have the potential to influence others to come together. You do, your friend does, your sister, your colleague, your client, your daughter.

Networker Connector women are engaging connection creators on a whole other level. The true connectors of the world. The Networker Connector in all of us will be better off for acknowledging this and drawing attention to how to honour your desire to be connected to self and others authentically. This is to live life fully and totally thriving. If you know your Thrive Factor Archetypes and know you are a Networker Connector, pay extra attention to these reflection prompts. Use them any time you're feeling the need to get out in the world and attend yet another event. Use them when you feel discomfort or uneasy spending time alone and connecting with yourself. Use them to support you to recognise the value you have as a woman who has a large community around her and how important it is you receive benefit from the community as much as they receive from you. If you don't yet know your Archetypes or are unsure if you are a Networker Connector you can 100% benefit from these reflections. We each have parts of all 12 Thrive Factor Archetypes within us, so a month of Networker Connector inspired reflections will certainly be exciting and freeing for you.

- **Who do I need to connect with for my own benefit?**
- **How can I be fully and completely myself in any given situation?**
- **What could I do for myself to be comfortable in my own space, alone and without others around?**
- **How can I teach others how to be more relaxed when meeting, mingling, and networking with others?**
- **Who do I know whom I would like to build a stronger or deeper relationship with so as to leverage that for our mutual gain in the future?**
- **How can I give to myself so as to be reminded of the value I offer to others?**

- In what ways can my business benefit from the community I have created?
- What is the reason I feel compelled to connect these people?
- What is my real truth and how do I show that to myself and to others?
- What makes me an individual and how can I celebrate that?
- What activities, other than connecting and being with people, can I gain energy from?
- How can I support myself to say no when I know it is the best answer to give?
- What consequences exist from my (often excessive) socialising?
- What ways do others like to be connected? Hint: ask them!
- In what ways can I stay visible in a crowd?
- Before going to an event ask yourself 'who is going to be there that I would like to meet and who do I know who knows this person or these people?'
- What about spending time connecting with myself makes me feel uncomfortable?
- How much do I value self connection?
- What suffers or misses out when I spend a lot of time attending events and networking?

afformations

The Networker Connector's afformations are designed to expand self connection, opening you to trust the value in your extensive network and open to see that value reflected back to you when you ask for and welcome the same kind of support you so effortlessly give to others – personally and professionally. Working with afformations creates expansion and a dynamic that opens you to experiencing even more celebration. When you ask the right questions and get playful with discovering answers for them, anything is possible. Afformations are fabulous for journaling, visualisation or meditation prompts or simply for reflecting.

- **What if time on my own was filling up my energy reserves?**
- **What if the value in my network was beautifully reflected to me by asking for help and support when I need it?**
- **What if staying home was a gift?**
- **What if saying no to others led to so many benefits because I understood it also meant saying yes to me and what I need most right now?**
- **What if I had an infinite well of value within me?**
- **What if my world was a safe place to ask for what I need?**
- **What if I could trust others would support me as much as I freely support and encourage them?**
- **What if I could abundantly enjoy all that quite time with self had to offer instead of wondering what I was missing out on?**
- **You could create more afformations of your own to embrace the Networker Connector themes.**

creative exercise

Connected Me with the themes of Self Connection, Self Value and Self Awareness

Reading through this chapter I am sure it is clear to you that our Networker Connector, the social butterfly of the Archetypes is fabulous at being the life of the party. Significantly to the detriment to her self connection a large percentage of the time. This month's creative exercise is valuable to you whether you identify with being an extrovert (common in true Networker Connectors) or introverted.

Time with and for self can be challenging to prioritise at any time and for all women. Show yourself how valuable you are to you and you'll reap the rewards for a long time to come. The Connected Me creative exercise is about welcoming more alone time into your schedule across the days and weeks of this month. It is learning to say no when your instinct is to say yes to an external invitation or request. It is becoming aware of how important self time is for you to be the kind of woman you desire to be in the world.

your creative exercise invitation

Activating the Connected Me creative exercise isn't one of lots of steps.

It is simple deliberately. All you are invited to do is to block out some time each day this month and practice self reflection and self connection any way that feels interesting and nourishing for you. Here are some examples you could try.

Do what you want to do, it is your self connection in focus here, not someone else's.

- Journal for 5 or 10 mins to start your day and set your intentions
- Begin a gratitude practice where you record at least 5 things you are grateful for to close off your day
- Take up meditation, or visualisation if your mind, like mine, responds to active prompts instead of trying to be quiet and empty
- Learn a breathwork process
- Try tapping and run through an EFT (emotional freedom technique) at least once a day to release what's not supporting you and welcome in more you time filled with abundance, self love, self value and self appreciation
- Do something that brings you back into your body and out of your busy, overthinking mind
- Sit in the park and watch the world pass by
- Take a power nap
- Go to bed earlier and read a chapter of a book that supports self connection

- Enjoy energy work like reiki, sound healing or meditation to bring you into the present
- Say no to the external and yes to you
- Do something creative as this will activate the psychological state of flow which is a divine expression of self connection
- Light a candle and watch the flame flicker for a few minutes without doing anything else
- Turn off your phone and sit in nature, absorbing all the energy the earth has to offer you.

Thrive Tip: When you feel any level of discomfort giving yourself more you time, sit with the discomfort. Allow it to rise up, notice it, acknowledge it, understand it is likely being driven by your ego and mind, and then invite it to pass.

NETWORKER CONNECTOR
SELF-CELEBRATION CHART

this month I...

Gave myself time and space to connect with myself	★★★★☆
Said no to an event invitation because I prioritised doing something for me	★★☆☆☆
Honoured the value of the network I have created	★★★☆☆
Reached out to one or more people to ask for support for something for myself	★☆☆☆☆
Paused before saying yes to every invitation because FOMO is not driving me!	★★★☆☆
Added quiet reflective time into my schedule to create greater balance in the busy	★☆☆☆☆
Recognised how valuable those I know are to my broader network	★★★☆☆
Spent time doing things I love solo	★★★★☆
Recognised the parts of me who aren't always so enthusiastic and listened to them	★★☆☆☆
Journaled using the Networker Connector prompts to gain deeper self connection	★★☆☆☆

Sign up for a year of Bragaudacious self celebration at www.thethrivefactor.com/bragaudacious

self-celebration from around the world

"Bath, French champagne, French cheese, massages, getting someone else to cook!"

 Chenae Carey, Brisbane, QLD, Australia

"We believe in EVERY business win - big, small or in between - should be shared, heard and celebrated! Win's create momentum – and show others what's possible. FOR THEM! Each week in the our Social Club Membership private Facebook group we ask our members to share their wins in business. As a small business owner, it's important to celebrate these wins because often we get so caught up in the hurricane of working in your business and your constantly growing to-do list, that you forget to stop and reflect on your achievements and how far you have come"

 Brooke Vulinovich, Perth, WA Australia

"I love to celebrate by surrounding myself with other beautiful souls so we can share, acknowledge and reflect on what we do. To me this gives me the ideal opportunity to not only recognise my own accomplishments but also be inspired by those around me, which is perfectly aligned with my amazing Inspirer Believer!"

 Michelle Daw, Perth, WA, Australia

"I celebrate from the smallest win to the most amazing high goals. One of my favourite celebrations is treating myself to lunch with my friends to raise my spirit or taking a day off for energy healing to recharge. Sometimes my celebration is simply allowing myself to just do exactly what my body feels like doing that day and doing it"

 Teniele Arnold, Perth, WA, Australia

"A celebration of powerful healing! At the age of 49 I learnt to celebrate my dwindling menstrual cycle. I hated my womb space for not working how she should have!! SHE should have created a child, but she gave me pain and misery called unexplained infertility, Endometriosis and PMDD.

My determination to thrive taught me to LOVE her and celebrate her in every phase of my menstrual cycle. She inspires me activating my Inspirer Believer in her Spring Follicular phase. She has my Shapeshifter Alchemist sexy a$$ moving in her unique magical way in Summer Ovulation. She has no say when my Mediator Diplomat (MD) steps up in my Autumn Luteal phase. MD screams at me to slow the F#@k down, where the F@#k is the balance.

Oh MD, you can be such a party pooper, but I celebrate MD nurturing me through my Luteal shadow phase, MD has my back or womb I should say. What comes next? The greatest celebration, my Winter Menstruation and who journeys and celebrates with me?

My Mentor Teacher who opens up to the divine wisdom that flows with menstrual blood, my Liberator Engineer allows me the space and freedom to be me and relax as I connect and celebrate the wisdom and focus of my womb as she releases the joys and sorrows of my last month!"

 Jane Hall, Canberra, ACT, Australia

Month Nine

PIONEER SEEKER

archetype themes

Exploration, Innovation, Disruption, Self treasure, Curiosity, Inclusivity, Originality, Self acceptance

goddess inspiration

Persephone

This month we take inspiration from the Pioneer Seeker, the ninth of the 12 Thrive Factor Archetypes. She is the Archetype of innovation and disruption. She's the one who will always push the boundaries and wants to forge into the world with a pioneering, going first sense of adventure and curiosity.

A woman of firsts, the Pioneer Seeker dreams of fitting in and being welcomed for being herself yet creates a whole load of experiences that highlight how different she really is. She can be a duality of extremes and what she says she wants and what she does can be in opposition to each other from an external point of view. She is critical, cheeky, sassy, judgemental when she's bored and easily distracted. These traits are directed at herself first but can be taken personally by others who may feel offended with what and how a Pioneer Seeker shares her views. That is another thing Pioneer Seekers will add to their list of things that activate boredom.

She can be so determined to prove a point and make her own way that she can get distracted from her mission and this can activate the external justification inherent in the Pioneer Seeker. This external justification is the Seeker expression. What's she seeking? To recognise she is a part of a world where she feels like an alien. To be seen, heard, and recognised for her differences. To know she is treasure. The treasure she seeks outside of her is always within. Turn inwards and the magic is right there waiting for you. No chaos needed. No disruption on the card. No changing things for the sake of it required.

Self leadership and acknowledgement of her value and differences is something every Pioneer Seeker can embrace with gusto, even if it feels uncomfortable. Acknowledging the energy, she has within that is linked to the Queen of the Underworld, the dark Queen energy is a significant gift. If you wish to understand this archetypal dynamic more search for the story of Greek maiden goddess Persephone for, she is the representation of this story. Meeting her will support you to understand this dynamic within yourself – how you can feel like one minute you are the helpless maiden and then the next minute you are a badass Queen. It is an interesting thing to see play out in the bold Pioneer Seekers I know.

The Pioneer Seeker, as you have discovered is, like all 12 Thrive Factor Archetypes, present in every woman. She may not actively be part of your Thrive Factor profile, but she exists within you in some way. She is the part of you who gets annoyed by societies demands to fit in. She is the part of you who gets bored easily and finds the path the masses follow to be incredibly distasteful and unengaging. She is the part of you who knows she is different and has felt left out most of her life. She is the part of you who tires of everyday things and wants constant adventure and fresh, original experiences all the time.

She is also the part of you who can easily deny your innovative ways and judge them unfairly. She is the part of you quick to dismiss things that others propose because they sound or feel boring. She is the part of you who starts everything with a disruption or creating chaos, often through boredom, sometimes as a distraction to push others away from the attention they are placing on you, no matter the reason for that attention.

She is the part of you who finds yourself wanting to fit in while maintaining your originality. You want to be accepted for who you are, but first must realise self acceptance, self value and self celebration are the route to external validation in the way you seek it. She is the part of you who is sassy, bold, a leader, a guide for others wanting a different way, a true pioneer charting her own path in the world, on her terms. Always on her terms. She's a big personality, an individual who challenges things, who believes her way is better because it's unique, who can be quick to judge others who she deems aren't that exciting. She's allergic to vanilla and if everyone else seems to be saying the sky is orange, she's going to be the one saying it's actually blue. She makes others laugh but will benefit so much from dropping the destructive joker vibe and welcoming her power.

the pioneer seeker's greatest gift to give herself is self acceptance

What is self acceptance?

- It is recognising there is nothing – absolutely, not one thing – that is evidence of you being broken or unvaluable in the world
- It is celebrating all parts of yourself, even if they have felt like the source of pain
- It is acknowledging your original and unique way of looking at things is wanted and needed
- It is being able to say that you have an infinite well of treasure within you and then to share that with the world
- It is to pause before you say or do something that comes from boredom as opposed to an opportunity to challenge the status quo productively
- It is welcoming others into your space, your heart, your entire world, and all areas of your life who will reflect to you how appreciated and valued you are for being you
- It is being unapologetically you – there is nothing to apologise about your ways, thoughts, values, beliefs, and drives.

pioneer seeker and self celebration

With your disruptive energy, frequent chaos and questioning your value you can often find yourself in situations that become a detriment of your personal wellbeing, every Pioneer Seeker within can be resistant to self celebration.

This month, to honour the parts of you that are

Disruptive, Original, Innovative, Adventurous, Determined,
Leading and Accepting

This is your invitation to spend time taking care of yourself in ways that feel like you're truly caring for you!

Being an inclusive self valuing and honouring woman is something your inner Pioneer Seeker will be wise to learn. It's not always the easiest thing for a Pioneer Seeker to do. It is possibly not the easiest thing for you to do either, whether you are a Pioneer Seeker or not.

- You find yourself abandoning what makes you who you are in order to create some unrealistic sense of fitting in
- You find yourself disrupting things for yourself and others because there has been too much flow and ease – while counter productive, this comes from mistrust of yourself, your potential and also from mistrust of others motives
- You find yourself spending an insane amount of time looking, seeking external justification of your value in the world
- You find yourself deciding you don't belong and abandoning whatever you are working on
- You find yourself denying the value of your unique perspectives.

You find yourself saying (often only to yourself for fear of being considered not valuable enough or too disruptive) "I just want to be seen and accepted for who I am" even though the words you hear come from your inner drive are saying "you're a rock goddess" or "you have everything you need" or "remember the Queen you are and go do whatever you darn well want!".

to celebrate yourself is to

- Understand your treasure is infinite and found within
- Show how you think and respond differently to the masses
- Find other Pioneer Seeker and Visionary Creator women for they are understanding of your position and want companionship without the fear of sharing their lane with too many others
- Tap into all the wisdom and value you have spent a lifetime collecting and acknowledge its value in your life and work
- Recognise your differences and let them drive you to be more you
- Give your inner dark Queen some space to lead on her own terms
- Resist the push to change things because you feel bored – sit in the boredom and let it pass
- Find ways to express your originality
- Ignore the screaming inside your head that says, "I can't do this because (insert whatever reason shouts the loudest)" and move forward trusting the decisions you've made and action you have taken were in your best interests
- Find the voice that has original opinions and let it lead you forward in alignment
- Take up all the space you desire to take up, in an unapologetic way
- Do something that feels so avante garde and boundary pushing because it's your truth.

reflection prompts

If you've travelled this book in chapter order you will have seen in other chapters that I have shared how one way to gain insight into who you are and to tune into the parts of you to be celebrated – and there are so many of them! – is to do active reflection. These prompts could be used as a theme for journaling, for meditation, for an art practice, or as a discussion topic with a friend or even in a sisterhood circle. This month, the second in your year of self celebration, continue to create regular time in your schedule for active reflection.

It is such a nourishing and expansive gift for all women to do in ways that honour who you innately are in the world. Each Thrive Factor Archetype has her own ways to reflect. Engaging with the monthly reflection prompts will provide you with insight into how you can use this month's Archetype to support wholistic reflection so as to gain insight and, if it arises, make choices and take action in line with what makes sense and you know is best for you.

The Pioneer Seeker brings reflection to how self accepting and valuing of your uniqueness you truly are

She offers you opportunity for inner connection to your sense of individuality and originality and to see these qualities are what makes you a treasured individual in the world, not the off one out as you may have experienced all your life. The Pioneer Seeker is innately wired to experience and create innovation and originality in the world, for herself and others. This, like the gifts of the other Thrive Factor Archetypes is something that is often dismissed by women. You are a true disruptor and driver of originality, whether you recognise and celebrate that fact or not. All women have the potential to influence their freedom. You do, your friend does, your sister, your colleague, your client, your daughter. Pioneer Seeker women are engaging innovators on a whole other level. The true liberators of the world. The Pioneer Seeker in all of us will be better off for acknowledging this and drawing attention to how to honour your need to craft an original path in the world, being your truly unique, fascinating, unrivalled self. This is so as to live life fully and totally thriving.

If you know your Thrive Factor Archetypes and know you are a Pioneer Seeker, pay extra attention to these reflection prompts. Use them any time you're feeling the need to break free, to break things before you break down, to define solutions, when you're into analytical mode and overanalysing and over engineering everything, when you crave ease and effortlessness. Use them when you're craving space and freedom. Use them to nurture your liberation fuelled heart that believes every soul deserves to know what it is to be free of whatever real and perceived limits, blocks, restrictions and patterns hold them back.

If you don't yet know your Archetypes or are unsure if you are a Pioneer Seeker you can beautifully benefit from these reflections. We each have parts of all 12 Thrive Factor Archetypes within us, so a month of Pioneer Seeker inspired reflections will certainly be exciting and honouring for you.

- How can I be content with the gifts I do have and accept they are the keys to unlock the most confident, empowered version of myself?

- What have I learned about taking risks and doing things first that I can use to support myself and others to push beyond their fears?

- What is the tangible evidence I have that tells me I am valuable, gifted and worthy?

- Within the adversity I have faced, what are the positives in relation to what I have learnt about my own strength and abilities?

- How can I remember to look within for the answers and solutions I naturally look for externally?

- How can I get support to follow through and to come to the end of my seemingly endless journey to be content with who I am?

- What does it mean to me to be a confident, mature woman and how can I embrace that?

- What are the positive things I have discovered about myself during times of adversity, depression or despair?

- How can I stand on my own two feet fully and completely?

- What can I do to support myself to take responsibility for who I am and the action I take, whilst continuing to have fun and be playful?

afformations

The Pioneer Seeker's afformations are designed to expand self honouring, opening you to trust your self and sense of adventure while also honouring the treasure you seek is already within you and not to be found in some out there distant space, place and time. This applies both personally and professionally. Working with afformations creates expansion and a dynamic that opens you to experiencing even more celebration. When you ask the right questions and get playful with discovering answers for them, anything is possible. Afformations are fabulous for journaling, visualisation or meditation prompts or simply for reflecting.

- **What if the treasure I seek externally is available to me in abundance on the inside?**
- **What if my disruptive ways to engage with the world are valuable to others?**
- **What if my unique, original views, thoughts and ways of expressing myself were the source of my superpowers?**
- **What if being an innovative woman gave me a genuinely unique approach to contributing the way I desire to?**
- **What if I had everything, I ever thought I needed and believed was missing?**

- What if I was the treasure, I have searched my whole life for?

- What if I could trust my instincts and believe there exist to serve and support me to make the difference I want to make?

- What if there was power and drive within me and it was effortless to tap into this infinite renewable resource at any time?

- You could create more afformations of your own to embrace the Pioneer Seeker themes.

creative exercise

My Personal Treasure Chest with the themes of Self Acceptance, Self Acknowledgement and Self Value

Ok superstar, rock goddess, push the boundaries woman, this is your time to stop looking outside in the world to attempt to fit in. You are a rebel, an innovator, a disruptor of boredom, allergic to vanilla, going the opposite way to the masses. All of what makes you, you, is valuable and will be acknowledged when you first acknowledge it – all of it – all of you – in your own honouring way.

your creative exercise invitation

As you like to do things your way and will likely not follow any suggestions or guidelines as to how that I could share here take this as permission to turn whatever you want into a container that can become your own Personal Treasure Chest.

In this treasure chest you can place things, words, thoughts, memories of experiences – anything that recognises your differences and reminds you that the more you, that you are, the better for you, for me, for us all. You are a woman who can rely on evidence and proof of your value, so this is your opportunity to create that. Have fun. Be your cheeky, sassy self. Be the Queen of the underworld you truly are. Lead your life, your work, your business, on your terms. Unbothered. Unapologetically. So badass!

Thrive Tip: Keep adding to your Personal Treasure Chest and every now and then go diving in to remember one of your growing number of treasures. Use that treasure the same day. This is celebrating all you are, in the moment. YES to more of that.

PIONEER SEEKER
SELF-CELEBRATION CHART

this month I...

Filled my Personal Treasure Chest with an abundance of evidence of all I am	★★★★☆
Looked within for answers	★★☆☆☆
Resisted believing my value is measure by the external in my world	★★★☆☆
Honoured and indulged my inner dark Queen anyway she desired	★☆☆☆☆
Listened to my instincts, knowing they guide and lead me for me	★★★☆☆
Recognised how much my inner world is full of opportunity, acted from that space	★☆☆☆☆
Opened to the see the gifts and wisdom within the whirlwind I create	★★★☆☆
Shared my uniqueness and quirks with the world instead of trying to fit in	★★★★☆
Understood how my unique ways of viewing the world are so valuable	★★☆☆☆
Let myself dress and express myself how I have always wanted to	★★☆☆☆

Sign up for a year of Bragaudacious self celebration at www.thethrivefactor.com/bragaudacious

self-celebration from around the world

"I'm a happy dancer. There's nothing quite like the expression of joyous celebration powerfully flowing through your body"

 Louise O'Reilly, Perth, WA, Australia

"As a Heroine Adventurer one of my go to celebrations is camping. I love to get out into nature and off the grid. The bigger the celebration the longer the stay!

My Shapeshifter Alchemist loves to celebrate by getting witchy. A new oracle deck, lighting the fancy candles ;), or a statement piece for my wardrobe. You never know when something with lots of flair will be perfect for a photoshoot!

My Pioneer Seeker loves to celebrate by doing something new or going somewhere I've never been. A new restaurant or inventing a new meal or fermenting something weird LOL.

Of course, my Visionary Creator just wants to play and get messy! So we celebrate by getting crafty. Getting out the paints, crayons, whatever, putting on some good tunes and having a fun go of it. Recently I celebrated a small win by trying cross-stitch for the first time... of course it's a sassy one.

The best is a combo, heading into nature, arts and crafts in tow, a good book, and even better food!"

 Stasha Washburn, USA

"I have such trouble with this!! Seriously, it's like asking "how do you breathe?" I notice, savour and celebrate the small things in my life and business. The big successes are just the accumulation of all the tiny milestones and wins along the way that I have already noticed and given thanks (gratitude) for. How do I celebrate- with deep and heartfelt gratitude for all the strengths in myself and others that added up to success"

 Jenny Cole, Perth, WA, Australia

"I ground my feet in the sand and allow the waves to flow over my feet and watch them disappear. My soul sends out messages of gratitude and thanks. I run along the beach just before day break and audibly converse with the Universe, expressing my blessings and words of celebration and appreciation. I buy myself gifts, pop a bottle of bubbly and cheers the life I live. I give thanks every morning before my eyes open and every night when my eyes close. Life is a gift and I have been given another day to celebrate it"

 Colleen Longstaff, Coffs Harbour, NSW, Australia

"My favourite way to celebrate would be to sit in the sunshine, overlooking a stunning water view, pop an ice cold bottle of bubbles and share it with the people who contributed to the success, reminiscing on the journey, all while getting a foot massage too"

 Ashley Matkovic, Perth, WA, Australia

Month Ten
QUEEN RULER

archetype themes

Quality, Leadership, Beauty, Expansion, Accomplishment, VIP Experiences, Regal, Luxury, Sovereignty, Compassion, Rulership

goddess inspiration

Oya

This month we take inspiration from the Queen Ruler, the tenth of the 12 Thrive Factor Archetypes. She is the Archetype of compassionate leadership and self rulership. She's always up for living with a bit (or a lot) of luxury and enjoying the finer things life has to offer as she moves forward leading her growing empire.

A compassion fuelled individual, she's here to create an impact and will champion success for herself and others. She uses her innate strengths to mobilise growth and loves to accomplish things. She's loyal and that loyalty extends to the individuals in the world she trusts most. Her inner circle is small and treasured, and often showered with gratitude for the Queen Ruler often knows what it is to have her loyalty and support abused.

She can be so focused on leading and growing her ambition infused great impact that she can become swayed by the ego of leadership. This often arises when a Queen Ruler feels threatened by another or others. Instead of inclusively leading with compassion and generosity, which is her innate tendency, she can fall into feeling a sense of threat, like there is a beheading coming soon. To understand this archetypal expression, think of the evil Queens you have met thanks to the Disney movies that have been present in pop culture across many generations. This evil Queen off-with-your-head energy is that of the shadow of the Queen Ruler. An egoistic Queen Ruler can create an instant repellent to those of her followers who love the generous, kind, compassionate and inclusive woman they have come to know and adore.

A Queen Ruler who senses threat can also get in first and control the situation by removing people and things from her world, literally beheading those who are not, in her opinion at the time, aligned. Rarely will she go back and admit if she has done this wrongly. She's moved on already and not given it another thought. I often say for this aspect of the Queen Ruler, it is a fabulous thing it is not a solo Archetype in any woman's Thrive Factor Profile.

Her love of the red carpet, VIP, luxurious life is something the Queen Ruler can struggle with. She can find the dichotomy of her desire and her reality tricky to balance, blend and accept. A Queen Ruler wants the top tier quality experience and the sooner she accepts and honours that the better. She is not materialistic by nature and would rather wait and have one of the best she can buy than have many things. She also relishes experiences and times with those she loves for these can truly feel luxurious and regal for her.

As a true lover of beauty and beautiful things and people, the Queen Ruler has a gift for design, and she shares this through her expression of self in the world. She loves to have just the right things in her orbit, creating her own sanctuary and castle wherever she goes. You'll feel special, beautiful, included, and pampered simply being within her space. Every woman loves a little bit of luxurious indulgence, and the Queen Ruler is your ideal partner in this. She is also quite phenomenal when it comes to celebration.

The Queen Ruler, as you learned with all 12 Thrive Factor Archetypes, is present in every woman. She may not actively be part of your Thrive Factor profile, but she exists within you in some way. She is the part of you who likes to be pampered. She is the part of you who is ambitious and appreciates the opportunity to lead and create community. She is the part of you who loves to support others with donations in a philanthropic way, which is different to that of the Advocate Rescuer. She is also the part of you who can get caught up in her own power and push forward to achieve on a large scale, often putting others offside on your way to the top. She wants loyalty but if ego is leading and not her heart, she can make others feel they have been pushed aside on her focused mission to make her impact in the world and be known for it.

She is the part of you who finds yourself wanting the very best, striving to achieve as an ambitious woman who is proud to claim she has goals and a desire to experience success, just like the Heroine Adventurer energy. Draw on her tenacity, her drive, her gift of inclusivity and her ability to bring others along for the experience. Take her innate leadership, grand vision and belief she has success in her destiny and use these traits to forge forward to create whatever you desire to create as an impact in your world. Leadership can be uncomfortable for many, but when you are surrounded by a trusted, loyal community who genuinely understand and support your vision, no matter its size, anything is possible. The Queen Ruler embodies this so beautifully.

the queen ruler's greatest gift to give herself is self rulership

What is self rulership?

- It is accepting and enjoying the kind of lifestyle and environment you truly desire to experience every day – denying it is ignoring who you are at your core
- It is making tough choices that are in favour of your desires and the greater good of all
- It is moving forward instead of ever getting caught in the emotional dimensions of decisions, relationships, and ego
- It is honouring your potential to lead on a large scale – you do not have to lead in a big way, but you can if you wish to

- It is being clear on the boundaries that are required to support and protect yourself from real and perceived threats so you can remain compassionate and generous
- It is understanding the true dynamic of leadership at the self level and continuing to nourish your personal leadership expression. Hint: the more you honour and allow yourself to express your Archetypes the greater your ability to authentically lead, beginning with personal leadership
- It is choosing your vision and taking action to turn it into actualised reality and building a supportive, inclusive, generously compassionate community along the way.

queen ruler and self celebration

With your vision for impact and desire to lead and create a life you adore, often to the detriment of your personal wellbeing, every Queen Ruler within can be resistant to self celebration.

This month, to honour the parts of you that are

Impactful, Regal, Leading, Compassionate, Inspired, Generous and Visionary

This is your invitation to spend time taking care of yourself in ways that feel like you're truly caring for you!

Being a generous, compassionate leader for herself is something your inner Queen Ruler will be wise to learn. It's not always the easiest thing for a Queen Ruler to do. It is possibly not the easiest thing for you to do either, whether you are a Queen Ruler or not.

- You find yourself falling into ego when challenged or threatened
- You find yourself moving onto the next thing without considering the impact of what you have just created or been involved in, ignoring the benefit of active acknowledgment and celebration
- You find yourself denying the kind of lifestyle you desire – this is often influenced by the combination of other Archetypes you have in your Thrive Factor Profile
- You find yourself quick to dismiss and move on from people you've decided don't measure up, or don't belong in your vision
- You find yourself keen to create beauty, harmony, luxury and yet frustrated these things can't just become reality instantly for you.

You find yourself saying (often only to yourself for fear of being considered unimportant and disrespected) "I have a big vision and wish to be supported" even though the words you hear come from your inner drive are saying "you are incredible" or "you are a leader others respect and are inspired by" or "your vision for the world is important and deserves to be recognised by many."

to celebrate yourself is to

- Give back to a cause that is meaningful and purposeful for you
- Pause before you make a quick decision and judgement and open to the well of compassion and generosity within
- Lighting a candle and taking a bath where you soak for as long as you feel
- Enjoying experiences that feel special, nourishing, indulgent, luxurious, no matter your current circumstances
- Letting yourself be taken care of by loved ones who want to pamper you in their own way
- Owning your leadership potential with enthusiasm
- Sharing your accomplishments with others
- Building nurtured relationships with your inner circle of trusted friends and confidantes
- Respect your desire for a top tier quality life experience and adding little things into your weeks to make this reality in your own unique way
- Take time to reflect on all you have accomplished, being in the moment and opening to see how incredible you are
- Buying fresh flowers for your home or office and luxuriating in the beauty of them
- Head to the day spa with your best girlfriends and enjoy any pampering that takes your fancy.

reflection prompts

If you've gorgeously moved this book in chapter order you will have seen in other chapters that I have shared how one way to gain insight into who you are and to tune into the parts of you to be celebrated – and there are so many of them! – is to do active reflection. These prompts could be used as a theme for journaling, for meditation, for an art practice, or as a discussion topic with a friend. This month, the second in your year of self celebration, continue to create regular time in your schedule for active reflection.

It is such a nourishing and expansive gift for all women to do in ways that honour who you innately are in the world. Each Thrive Factor Archetype has her own ways to reflect. Engaging with the monthly reflection prompts will provide you with insight into how you can use this month's Archetype to support wholistic reflection so as to gain insight and, if it arises, make choices and take action in line with what makes sense and you know is best for you.

The Queen Ruler brings reflection to how self led and compassionately leading you truly are

She offers you opportunity for inner connection to your sense of vision, beauty, desire to impact others positively and also to your wish to be a compassionate leader. The Queen Ruler is innately wired to experience and create beauty and impact in the world, for herself and others. This, like the gifts of the other Thrive Factor Archetypes is something that is often dismissed by women. You are a true compassionate, considerate leader, whether you recognise and celebrate that fact or not. All women have the potential to influence their lived experience and self leadership expression. You do, your friend does, your sister, your colleague, your client, your daughter. Queen Ruler women are enticing leaders on a whole other level. The genuine inclusive impact makers of the world.

The Queen Ruler in all of us will be better off for acknowledging this and drawing attention to how to honour your desire to be the regal, generous, caring, welcoming, beauty and luxury loving leader.

This is so as to live life fully and totally thriving. If you know your Thrive Factor Archetypes and know you are a Queen Ruler, pay extra attention to these reflection prompts. Use them any time you're feeling the need to be treated like the queen you are. Let them guide you to a greater sense of your leadership potential. Let them be a reflection of the quality you appreciate and deserve, across all things and experiences. Use them when you're craving a VIP and luxurious experience. Use them to nurture your generous, giving heart and to reflect back to you the natural compassion that will support you to release whatever real and perceived limits, blocks, restrictions and patterns hold them back.

If you don't yet know your Archetypes or are unsure if you are a Queen Ruler you can certainly benefit from these reflections. We each have parts of all 12 Thrive Factor Archetypes within us, so a month of Queen Ruler inspired reflections will certainly be exciting and freeing for you.

- **How can I be a genuine leader and lead with compassion as the primary driver?**
- **What do I need in order to lead my own life authentically; to be fully in my power?**
- **How can I stay wise and consistently make decisions and choices from the place of generous compassion instead of perceived threat, fear or scarcity?**
- **What is most important to me when it comes to my environment and how can I create the beauty and opulence that makes me feel safe, secure and content?**

- In what ways can I step more consistently into being the leader I have the potential to be?
- How can I lead my life with greater value, compassion and generosity for myself and for others?
- In what ways can I give back to demonstrate my generous spirit?
- How do I remind myself daily what is most important to me as a Queen Ruler?
- What does my environment need for me to feel secure and able to fulfill my innate potential?
- How can I stay powerful and confident without taking power away from others?
- What does it mean to me to trust myself and how can I do that?
- How can I show my vulnerable side without compromising myself and feeling weak or threatened?
- What is important to me in a friend and who do I know who is a real, genuine friend where we are equal in our relationship?
- How can I generously share value and beauty in the world without feeling taken advantage of?
- What is my definition of luxury and how can I include it in all I do without 'showing off'?
- Who challenges me the most? How do they challenge me and what can I do about the feelings that rise up when that happens?
- How can I stay grounded and real in my life and in my business while still honouring my royal place in the world?

afformations

The Queen Ruler's afformations are designed to expand self leadership, opening you to trust your leadership potential and express your regal qualities in all aspects of your expression in the world, both personally and professionally. Working with afformations creates expansion and a dynamic that opens you to experiencing even more celebration. When you ask the right questions and get playful with discovering answers for them, anything is possible. Afformations are fabulous for journaling, visualisation or meditation prompts or simply for reflecting.

- **What if the quality I love so much is also loved by those I spend time with?**
- **What if I have everything, I require to be the kind of leader I desire to be?**
- **What if in every moment it was easy for me to give myself the quality, I wish to experience in all my interactions?**
- **What if I was destined to be a success?**
- **What if I truly had the potential to create significant impact in the world by being 100% me?**
- **What if I was the source of my power?**
- **What if a red carpet life was one I experienced each day?**
- **What if my generous support of causes and people I believe in returned to me in beautiful rewards without expectation?**
- **You could create more afformations of your own to embrace the Queen Ruler themes.**

creative exercise

Queen For A Day with the themes of
Self Rulership, Self Sovereignty and Self Acceptance

Every woman loves to feel a sense of beauty, luxury, pampering and like she is indulging for no good reason. Really, who needs a reason to enjoy the finer things in life?

Queen Ruler women act on these desires with ease. The rest of us can find it more of a challenge to give to ourselves in this way. The creative exercise this month, inspired by the energy and presence of the Queen Ruler within every woman is to plan and live out being a Queen for the day. The sky is the limit here. Your Queen for a day experience can cost as little or as much as you like or have to spend.

There are no rules in this scenario. The Queen Ruler makes her own rule in every aspect of life, work and business. Always!

your creative exercise invitation

What to do:

Answer these following prompts to plan out your Queen for a day experience.

- What does luxury feel like for me?
- What things feel luxurious?
- What do I most desire to experience in terms of luxury and beauty now?
- What could I do to bring more luxury into my world now?
- What will I do to bring more luxury into my world this month?
- When will I live out my Queen for a day experience?
- Who will I invite to join me (totally optional)?
- How will I feel in every moment living out my Queen for a day experience?

The next step is to schedule it, invite anyone you want to share to with and then live it out, with the beautiful, indulgent energy of the Queen Ruler you have within you. Wear your crown with pride gorgeous soul.

Thrive Tip: Why not dedicate a day each month to embracing your inner Queen Ruler. When you do be sure to share on your socials and tag me in. You can find all my social media links at www.thrivefactorco.com/shannon-dunn-links. Oh, and use the hashtags #bragaudacious and #queenforaday so I can easily find your shares. Let's create a revolution of thriving anyway we can in the world. This is a gorgeous way to show others you are here to care for and honour yourself in a sovereign way, literally.

QUEEN RULER
SELF-CELEBRATION CHART

this month I...

Indulged in things that make me feel beautiful	★★★★☆
Took my dearest friends out for a special occasion to collectively celebrate us	★★☆☆☆
Donated to a cause that is purposeful for me	★★★☆☆
Added an item to my home or work environment that felt luxurious and indulgent	★☆☆☆☆
Took a bath at least weekly	★★★☆☆
Booked (and attended) a day spa!	★☆☆☆☆
Shared my vision with the world and welcomed the infinite support available to me	★★★☆☆
Owned my vision and took action to bring it to life, with support, each day	★★★★☆
Enjoyed my surroundings and loved time resting and nourishing my soul	★★☆☆☆
Wore my crown with pride *(Author note: many Queen Rulers I know actually have a crown or two and love wearing them!)*	★★☆☆☆

Sign up for a year of Bragaudacious self celebration at www.thethrivefactor.com/bragaudacious

self-celebration from around the world

"As a woman I had only ever thought about celebration in the sense of a birthday or an event or something that is always on the calendar. I have learnt that celebration is so much more than that my queen ruler archetype she dominates a lot of what I do (in a totally good way) that's allowed me to see that I do need to celebrate more.

For me celebration means that I've done something well that my hard work and dedication to a project has paid off, this comes in little steps with numbers reached milestones achieved and everything that goes into my business.

When I do celebrate, I do this with a commitment that what I'm doing is important. Within the celebration it gives me time to breathe and reflect on what I do and the path I'm here to walk. Taking time to breathe for me is vital because it is when I do not take a breath and I do not celebrate what I've done that I become burnt out and exhausted and not interested in what I'm doing"

 Liesel Albrecht, Traralgon, Victoria, Australia

"I celebrate small moments throughout the day, connecting me back to my Source and my purpose. These small celebrations remind me to love who I am. Welcoming the day with love and gratitude, joyfully acknowledging each accomplished task throughout the day, taking JOY breaks from work by closing my eyes and beaming joy to the world for 5 minutes, and ending my day in deep mediation"

 Dawn Taylor, Denver, Colorado, USA

"A few years back when I was a registered nurse and long before starting my business, I had to have a spinal fusion. I had to change my celebratory style for a while after surgery, as I couldn't jump, and I am a jump up and down get excited type of person. So I adapted, and I still do it to this day, we call it 'my happy dance". It is a funny dance where my feet are stuck to the ground (originally to protect my back) and I lift my arms up and in front and to the sides whilst I do a silly knee bend and wobble. It is quite a sight to behold, haha, and now even when I can jump up and down, I still do the happy dance"

 Michelle Rimmer, Perth, WA, Australia

"I think my method of celebration is sharing. When I have achieved something, I make it a moment for me and the people who got me there (because I rarely do things without support in the background, even if those people don't know it ;)). Last year I earned my Masters - we didn't get to have a graduation ceremony initially because of Covid. But the first thing I did was send pictures of my diploma to my family, friends and colleagues, sharing my achievement whilst acknowledging their place in my journey.

Generally, I don't feel like it's a celebration unless I am celebrating with someone else or others.

Celebration is about sharing the moment with the ones you love. It doesn't have to be bells and whistles, just lots of love and appreciation"

 Stephanie Powell, Perth, WA, Australia

Month Eleven
SHAPESHIFTER ALCHEMIST

archetype themes

Magic, Transformation, Flexibility, Visibility, Adaptability, Manifestation

goddess inspiration

Isis

This month we take inspiration from the Shapeshifter Alchemist, the eleventh of the 12 Thrive Factor Archetypes. She is the Archetype of magic and transformation. She's always excited by the possibility of some intriguing, mystical experience and adores recognising her own magic within the realms of transformation.

A true alchemist, she possesses the gift of transformation in an authentic alchemical way. Her very presence can be the catalyst for evolving something or someone of seemingly little or no value into something of incredible wealth and prosperity. This is not a money related expression at all. It is a whole life and whole being expression that she can find challenging to accept and use for the benefit of herself and others.

She is the chameleon of the Thrive Factor Archetypes and effortlessly weaves, changes and evolves. She needs flexibility, fluidity, and safety to transform as needed. She can, when she allows herself, genuinely understand what it is like to walk in another individuals' shoes, for she can imagine, in her magical way, exactly what that would be like. This attribute is appreciated by others who are grateful for her expansive sense of compassion and understanding and willingness to support them as needed. It is incredibly important she nurtures these qualities and uses them to remain visible and expressing herself in the world.

Shapeshifter Alchemist can be so unaware of her potential and the mystery she exudes in the world that she can struggle to create a sense of safety. She desires to feel and know she is safe and welcomed before she will let herself fully express in all the magical ways she has the potential to. The depth of her magic is infinite. To her magic is the very essence of being. It is not trinkets, and those things others may perceive as magical. To a Shapeshifter Alchemist magic can be found anywhere. The faster she acknowledges and celebrates this the better her magic can support her in the world where she can often feel that hiding is the best solution to the reality she is experiencing.

Due to the influence of her other Archetypes the Shapeshifter Alchemist can, at times, feel disconnected from the gifts of this Archetype. She can find the magic within at odds with other aspects of herself that are more grounded, analytical, and critical. This can see her experiencing an interesting dance with this aspect of herself which can, at times, feel easier to deny than to embody. Embodying this Archetype is her first step to full self expression, maximising the strengths and gifts of all her Archetypes, no matter how many she has. Welcoming magic into her day every single day is so important for this Archetype. No matter what it is, as long as it creates a sense of magic for the Shapeshifter Alchemist, she is enhancing her wellbeing on every level. She is wise to include ritual in her days and weeks, months and years. It may be as simple as using afformations, journaling to start her day, a gratitude practice, lighting a candle, creating and nurturing an alter in a sacred place at home, conversations with her magical sisterhood. Anything that nourishes her soul is valuable and will ground her sense of self and wellbeing, magically of course.

The Shapeshifter Alchemist, as you learned in previous chapters is, like all 12 Thrive Factor Archetypes, present in every woman. She may not actively be part of your Thrive Factor profile, but she exists within you in some way. She is the part of you who is intrigued by the mysteries of being a woman. She is the part of you who loves the magic she finds in the world. She is the part of you who can guide others evolutionary transformation for herself and others. She is intriguing, colourful, whimsical, mystical and here to alchemise that which is not useful into something of immense value. She is also the part of you who can feel lost and unvalued in the world. The part of you who feels out of place and uncertain about the safety of being visible and truly showing who she is to those in her life. She is the part of you who can hide aspects of self because there never seems to be the right time or place to share them with the greater population. So hidden she often stays.

She is the part of you who desires to create change, to transform in ways that cannot be explained. Welcome the magic within you and around you and celebrate it boldly and with gratitude. It exists in every woman and when acknowledged it can be expanded and used for the transformation wished for. Be mindful of your thoughts, words, feelings, and actions as much as possible so you can positively influence your gift for manifestation. What you think, say, feel and do can become your reality at an intensely fast speed. This is something to enjoy and trust as your truth. Just as this can be something that brings unwanted things into your life, you have the ability to change things around quickly and sustainably.

the shapeshifter alchemist's greatest gift to give herself is self transformation

What is self transformation?

- It is recognising and celebrating that you are ever changing
- It is understanding that there is nothing about you that needs to be changed because it is wrong, broken or unworthy and instead transforming is your personal evolution and becoming
- It is integrating the shadow as the powerful wisdom of your past
- It is being open to spreading your wings and feeling free and visible in the world
- It is knowing you are safe to be seen and your magic is desired by others
- It is embracing your gift for guiding others through their own transformations as you walk your own evolution
- It is choosing YOU as a mystic, the alchemist with a gift for manifestation.

shapeshifter alchemist and self celebration

With your journey of finding your place in the world, feeling safe and secure and valued exactly as you are, often to the detriment of your personal visibility and evolution, every Shapeshifter Alchemist within can be resistant to self celebration.

This month, to honour the parts of you that are

Curious, Magical, Evolving, Expressive, Colourful,
Transforming and Mystical

**This is your invitation to spend time taking care of yourself
in ways that feel like you're truly caring for you!**

Being magic for herself is something your inner Shapeshifter Alchemist will be wise to learn. It's not always the easiest thing for a Shapeshifter Alchemist to do. It is possibly not the easiest thing for you to do either, whether you are a Shapeshifter Alchemist or not.

- You find yourself falling into hiding when you are uncertain
- You find yourself denying how valued and appreciated you are to believe this is a way to create safety
- You find yourself avoiding the things that nourish you because you feel they are not welcomed by others
- You find yourself desiring experiences that do not seem to fit within your every day life

- You find yourself wanting to feel more grounded, accepted, considered interesting and valuable.

You find yourself saying (often only to yourself for fear of being considered unorthodox or unacceptable) "I want to be comfortable being who I am" and "I feel unsure about my place in the world and how to be me" or "I am so different to others, so how can I ever be accepted?"

to celebrate yourself is to

- **Understand your desire to be your authentic self is a gift that will amplify for the entire of your lifetime**
- **Create space to nourish your personal evolution**
- **Learn that your uniqueness is wanted and needed in the world**
- **Take time to honour the flexibility and change that you need as you learn exactly who you are**
- **Acknowledge the importance of magic**
- **Celebrate your visibility as a sign you have accepted and nurtured your gifts and strengths**
- **Allow yourself to be visible, to be seen**
- **Give gratitude to yourself for creating safety and sharing your magic with others after giving it to yourself first**
- **Drop the invisibility cloak and find ways and places to let yourself be celebrated for who you are**

- **Indulge in things that feel magical, mystical and unusual by others standards and judgements**
- **Let go of the limits manifesting has had for you and instead focus on the positives this has to offer when you are focused and considered of your thoughts, words, feelings and actions**
- **Expand into the world as the bright, colourful, intriguing chameleon you are.**

reflection prompts

If you've followed this book in chapter order you will have seen in other chapters that I have shared how one way to gain insight into who you are and to tune into the parts of you to be celebrated – and there are so many of them! – is to engage in active reflection. These prompts could be used as a theme or focus for journaling, for meditation, for an art practice, or as a discussion topic with a friend or even a sisterhood circle. This month, the eleventh in your year of self celebration, continue to create regular time in your schedule for active reflection. It is such a nourishing and expansive gift for all women to do in ways that honour who you innately are in the world. Each Thrive Factor Archetype has her own ways to reflect that will be beneficial. Engaging with the monthly reflection prompts will provide you with insight into how you can use this month's Archetype to support wholistic reflection so as to gain insight and, if it arises, make choices and take action in line with what makes sense and what you know is best for you.

The Shapeshifter Alchemist brings reflection to how self transformation plays a part in all areas of your life

She offers you opportunity for connection to your innate magic and gifts to evolve to live a life of greater abundance, richness and wealth on all levels if you desire. The Shapeshifter Alchemist is innately wired to experience transformation in the world, for herself and others. This, like the gifts of the other Thrive Factor Archetypes is something can be denied by women. You are a true mystic, whether you recognise and celebrate that fact or not. All women have the potential to influence their personal evolution. You do, your friend does, your sister, your colleague, your client, your daughter. Shapeshifter Alchemist women are mystical creators of magical experiences that lead to transformation on a whole other level. The Shapeshifter Alchemist in all women will be better off for acknowledging this and drawing attention to how to honour your joy of magical expression and the mystical gifts of being female. This is to live life fully and totally thriving.

- **What actions should I take to clearly see what needs to be done in order to achieve the outcome I am working towards?**
- **How can I use my ability to reinvent myself in order to discover the real me?**
- **What role does magic play in my life?**
- **Is there a way for me to use my natural gift for transformation in my life and the lives of others?**
- **How can I bring the magical things I love into my business?**
- **What will it take for me to be as visible as possible, trusting it is safe to let people into the parts of my world which I have previously hidden?**
- **How can I trust what I know and stay true to my inner voice, particularly when others are challenged by the conviction I have in my belief?**

- What are the things I love to offer the most in business?
- Where do these business offerings intersect and what opportunity exists in this intersection that can inform my future business offerings?
- How can I be consistent with my core messages so as to provide a reliable solution for others?
- How can I safely show the real me to the world?
- What is the real honest truth of who I am?
- As a business woman, or woman in leadership, what is the identity or brand I want to portray?
- How can I portray who I am consistently and resist the need to continually change who I am and what I offer?
- What other archetypes do I have and how can I use their strengths to ground me as a Shapeshifter Alchemist?
- How can I be truthful with myself about what is most important to me and the sides of me that the world deserves to know?
- What triggers and activations are there that tell me when I am getting caught up in the magic and being unrealistic about what I am entering into?
- Where can I create flexibility and variety in my life so I am not tempted to create too much of this in my business?
- What boundaries can I put in place to support me and still create the flexibility and variety I crave and need?

afformations

The Shapeshifter Alchemist's afformations are designed to expand self transformation, opening you to trust your magic and to guide you to express the gift of transformation you offer to all, in all your expressions in the world. Working with afformations creates expansion and a dynamic that opens you to experiencing even more celebration. When you ask the right questions and get playful with discovering answers for them, anything is possible. Afformations are fabulous for journaling, visualisation or meditation prompts or simply for reflecting.

- **What if my magic was my medicine?**
- **What if my personal transformation was an inspiration for all?**
- **What if being visible was safe for me at all times?**
- **What if I was valued for my differences and magical ways?**
- **What if manifesting what I truly desire was effortless and fun?**
- **What if I could use my strengths to positively influence my world and the world at large?**
- **What if I welcomed more magic into my life?**
- **What if I celebrated being the magical, mystical Queen of transformation?**
- **You could create more afformations of your own to embrace the Shapeshifter Alchemist themes.**

creative exercise

Gratitude for Magic with the themes of
Self Transformation, Self Flexibility and Self Visibility

With magic presenting as a significant theme for the Shapeshifter Alchemist Archetype it is fitting to focus the creative exercise for this shiny chameleon on amplifying your magic.

Every woman has her own magic and it's limited presence in her life is often as a result of denying it exists, or hiding it for some fear or concern of what it means or how others may judge it when expressed more freely.

Let's release those limits right now and get ready to express gratitude for the magic within and the amplification and expansion of that magic in the world, whatever form it takes. Who knows how it may be expressed, we are talking magic after all?

your creative exercise invitation

For this month get yourself a beautiful, colourful notebook, or section off an area of your journal for you are going to capture the magic you sense and see in each day for the entire month.

The exercise is a simple one. Make a new entry in your journal and respond to the following prompts.

For a morning practice, "Today I welcome magic in the following ways..."
For an evening practice, "Today I witnessed magic show up in the following ways..."

Add another prompt after your response to the morning or evening prompt and respond to "I am grateful for all the magic I see, experience, sense and know is present because..."

Over the month be mindful of what you experience and celebrate every aspect of magic that you become aware of. I get the sense it's going to be a true month of celebration and that is exactly what you are here for. Yes to more magic superstar!

At the end of each week reflect on what you have experienced and fill a page in response to "I am magic and these are all of the ways I celebrate magic in my life..."

SHAPESHIFTER ALCHEMIST
SELF-CELEBRATION CHART

this month I...

Tried something that felt magical more often than I ever have before	★★★★☆☆
Became aware of all the magic I have available to me	★★☆☆☆☆
Learned about manifestation	★★★☆☆☆
Put consideration into my thoughts, words, feelings and actions	★☆☆☆☆☆
Let go of unhelpful judgements I have had about magic and magical experiences	★★★☆☆☆
Celebrated being more visible and feeling safe	★☆☆☆☆☆
Completed the creative practice regularly during the month	★★★☆☆☆
Focused on the gifts of my differences in place of feeling out of place	★★★★☆☆
Let myself be more playful	★★☆☆☆☆
Welcomed learning about the various sides of me and all the contributions they offer	★★☆☆☆☆

Sign up for a year of Bragaudacious self celebration at www.thethrivefactor.com/bragaudacious

self-celebration from around the world

 "Every e-commerce order I receive the customer's name pops up on my screen so I offer my gratitude to my customers. I message thank you's to my customers when they send me photos of their tie dyes and testimonials as we're celebrating together. Recently I completed something that took me months to complete due to needing policies that I needed to develop for the program. I celebrated by purchasing a t-shirt I adore. I also celebrate everything with my business bestie and family."

Kimberlie Clare-Campbell, Maitland NSW Australia

"How do I celebrate myself as a woman? It has been a long journey for me to be able to celebrate myself as a woman in ALL my beautiful glory - appreciating all parts of me. Including all the intricate layers, the light, the shadow and every-thing in between. I now do this with ease and I am so proud of the woman that I have become - unapologetically me. I no longer have the need to be liked or accepted by all and knowing that I am perfectly imperfect the way that I am. Realising deep down in my heart and soul that the right people will love, support and celebrate me and most importantly that it starts with me appreciating and loving who I am. I am who I am and I can now say with wide open arms and a pure heart, this is me - you either like me or you don't, you either celebrate me or you don't.. No mask, pure authentically me, fierce yet gentle, compassionate and kind, yet now having strong healthy boundaries, loving, intuitive, wise and creative me. The woman that was hidden, suppressed and full of fear and misery for so long is now completely visible and not afraid to shine my light brightly, without restraint. I am a woman who is determined to make a difference and keep rising and celebrate who I am and who I am becoming"

 Jo Worthy, Canberra, ACT, Australia

"How do I celebrate? How ever the hell I want to.
I believe everything we do gets to come from a place of desire not should.

If I desire to celebrate by indulging in a lux experience- I will!
If I desire to celebrate by running. 5kms - I will!
If I desire to celebrate by hiding away from the world with a trashy tv show - I will!

Celebrate however YOU desire beautiful woman, for you are no-one else and that's your ticket to freedom."

 Nicky Thomas, Perth, WA, Australia

"I celebrate by
1. Giving big huge gratitude and thanks first up
2. giving myself something luxe, like a 90 minute spa treatment, go out to eat at a fab restaurant
3. Buy more art materials!!!! Whoop"

 Aesha Kennedy, Mullumbimby, NSW, Australia

Month Twelve
VISIONARY CREATOR

archetype themes

Knowing, Seeing, Creative Expression, Journeying, Futuristic, Visionary, Shamanic

goddess inspiration

Athena

This month we take inspiration from the Visionary Creator, the twelfth of the 12 Thrive Factor Archetypes and the last in the Thrive Factor alphabet. She is the Archetype of expression. She is the conduit between the future and the present and the way she thinks and engages with the world is often avant-garde, innovative and futuristic, although this may not always be obvious to those around her.

The creative soul of the Archetypes, she is the one most likely to have innate artistic talent. She creates compulsively and is an incredible expressive woman who others would abundantly describe as their creative friend. A lover of colour and artistic mastery, she expresses differently to the craft loving Inspirer Believer and natural designer Queen Ruler, although each of these Archetypes are considered creative in their own way. She may not initially identify as creative, getting caught up in societal beliefs that to be creative means to have natural artistic ability. She can be a true artist if she desires to be. Most important is she engages with self expression and creating in any way she feels drawn to. Like freedom is breathing to the Liberator Engineer, creating is breathing for the Visionary Creator.

She is a thinking woman and intelligence, and intellectual pursuits are important to her. She has a natural business acumen and is often interested in big business, leadership roles and entrepreneurship. Her gift for strategy serves her well in anything she undertakes from a career perspective. Her creative side is a balancer to the time she can spend in her head and, as with the Heroine Adventurer who benefits from time in nature to balance her intense fierce and focused traits, any kind of regular creative expression is essential for any Visionary Creator. Trust me, I know this all too well as this is one of my four Thrive Factor Archetypes. Everything is more likely to be in flow when I am actively creating and enjoying learning a new artistic skill, painting, writing poetry and doing this alongside the creating that happens as part of my business expression.

The Visionary Creator has an innate sense of knowing and she tends to trust the visions and messages she receives. She is incredibly intuitive and perceptive and will always benefit from investing time and energy to nurture this side of herself. She also has the ability for effortless manifestation, but in a different way to the Shapeshifter Alchemist. Her manifesting is in response to the energy she places in her visions – the things she sees are possible – and ensuring she values her instinct to trust in what she sees, she will find her futuristic, no specific timeline visions, will become her reality. To be clear though, this visionary aspect of her character is not like that of a clairvoyant. I laugh thinking of the number of times women have heard me talk about the visionary traits of this Archetype and sidled up to me hoping I will see something for them and share it. It doesn't work like that. I have learned to call up my visioning for myself on demand, but I have not mastered this for my clients, friends, or strangers. Not yet anyway!

The Visionary Creator, as you discovered with all 12 Thrive Factor Archetypes, is present in every woman. She may not actively be part of your Thrive Factor profile, but she exists within you in some way. She is the part of you who loves to express yourself. She is the part of you who is intuitive and trusts in her intuition, following her instincts and believing they can become reality. She is the part of you who loves her career and using her brain to progress forward for the benefit of herself and others.

She is also the part of you who can find herself intensely impatient, wondering when all your effort will pay off. She is the part of you who denies her creativity and dismisses it as a nice thing to do, as opposed to the gift it is for all women. She is the part of you who can over strategise and over control the outcome, trying too hard to turn that vision and dream of a certain future into reality now.

She's bold, she's wise, she's evolutionary, she's a creative soul and a woman often on a mission to make an impact. She is the one Archetype most likely to invent an original thing in the world and when she's patient with its reality, she will experience the most incredible success with seeming ease and effortlessness. The reality is, her vision may have first appeared to her some long ago time. Her tenacious belief in her vision and ability to take consistent action to bring it to life are admirable.

Her strength of connection to the future and ability to stay connected to the present moment is a true ability she will learn to value as she understands how much others value it. Earlier in 2021, 11 years after first crafting the Visionary Creator Archetype and with over a decade of observation of myself and the handful of other women I have met who are Visionary Creators (side note, she's so far, the least common Archetype from the thousand plus women I have personally profiled and coached!), I gained a whole new understanding of her power. I saw, in true Visionary Creator style, that she is attune to a shaman. This speaks to her ability to effortlessly journey with others into other times and spaces, mostly the future, to glean insight into the resources, gifts, insights and learning that is valuable in the present time. This still blows me away but I am learning to have fun with it and share that fun in my work.

the visionary creator's greatest gift to give herself is self expression

What is self expression?

- It is letting yourself show up in the world in ways that work for you
- It is playing with colour and allowing it into your life, your work, your clothing, all you do and who you are
- It is exploring creative expression and finding how you express yourself with ease
- It is being unbothered and unapologetic about who you are
- It is letting go of other people's observations and feedback about who you are and what you stand for in the world

- It is recognising that you can master artistic skill but knowing that your version of creative self expression may not be what you think it will be
- It is speaking your thoughts, beliefs and values and living in tune with them each day.

visionary creator and self celebration

With your strategic brain and connection to the future realms every Visionary Creator within can be uncertain about enjoying expressions from the perspective of self celebration.

This month, to honour the parts of you that are

Creative, Expressive, Colourful, Forward thinking, Strategic, Visionary and Trusting

This is your invitation to spend time expressing yourself in ways that feel expansive and creative for you

Becoming a lover of self expression is a generous gift your inner Visionary Creator will be benefit immensely from learning. It is innate to express, but not always the easiest thing for a Visionary Creator to do to the magnitude that this Archetype has the capacity to express creatively. It is possibly not the easiest thing for you to do either, whether you are a Visionary Creator or not.

- You find yourself falling into doubt and uncertainty as a default
- You find yourself resisting creativity because you have intellectual pursuits to engage with
- You find yourself feeling intensely impatient as you frustratingly wonder when your visions will become your reality
- You find yourself wanting ease and a joyous life but struggling with how to create this when you're stuck in strategy mode
- You find yourself wanting to trust more and know exactly what is possible in the present rather than being distracted by what can come to be in the future.

You find yourself saying (often only to yourself for fear of being considered untrustworthy and unrealistic) "I just want things to happen faster" even though the words you hear come from your inner drive are saying "create and have fun" or "be patient, it is all working out in divine timing" or "keep trusting."

to celebrate yourself is to

- **Know you are a creative woman at your core**
- **Express yourself in ways that nourish you and make you feel expansive and alive**
- **Honour the creative energy of being female and understand that to create is to express**
- **Let go of preconceived ideas and judgements about your creative expression**
- **Trust in your incredible gifts of intuition and open to more trust in what you know and see are possible**
- **Share the visions you have for your life, career or business with as many trusted souls as you can, knowing the collective expression will support your visions to become actualised**
- **Learn the art of patience and knowing that things are coming to be in the right timing for your bold vision**
- **Play with colour and expression in your clothes, home and any space you spend time in**
- **Buy yourself some art supplies and simply play with them**
- **Take a creative workshop or class and enjoy learning something new where you get to express your creativity**
- **See and honour yourself as a creative woman – literally use the word creative to describe yourself**
- **Have fun with intuition and manifesting because you never know what may come to be.**

reflection prompts

If you've followed this book in chapter order you will have seen in all other chapters that I have shared how one way to gain insight into who you are and to tune into the parts of you to be celebrated – and there are so many of them! – is to do active reflection. These prompts could be used as a theme for journaling, for meditation, for an art practice, or as a discussion topic with a friend. This month, the second in your year of self celebration, continue to create regular time in your schedule for active reflection.

It is such a nourishing and expansive gift for all women to do in ways that honour who you innately are in the world. Each Thrive Factor Archetype has her own ways to reflect. Engaging with the monthly reflection prompts will provide you with insight into how you can use this month's Archetype to support wholistic reflection so as to gain insight and, if it arises, make choices and take action in line with what makes sense and you know is best for you.

The Visionary Creator brings reflection to how self expressive and trusting in your knowing you truly are

She offers you opportunity for exploring the depth of your intuition and the development of this innate feminine gift. She is here to show you that your intellect and strategic mind can be used to create powerful, impactful things that benefit so many others, starting with yourself. The Visionary Creator is innately wired to express creatively and bring the resources, insights and learnings of the future to the present, for herself and others. This, like the gifts of the other Thrive Factor Archetypes is something often dismissed by women. You are a true visionary and creative, whether you recognise and celebrate that fact or not. All women have the potential to influence their future. You do, your friend does, your sister, your colleague, your client, your daughter. Visionary Creator women are enticing creators on a whole other level. The true creatives of the world. The Visionary Creator in all of us will be better off for acknowledging this and drawing attention to how to honour your desire to be and reality you are driven by a need for creative expression as a means to connect to clarity of vision as much as you need oxygen to breath. This is so as to live life fully and totally thriving.

If you know your Thrive Factor Archetypes and know you are a Visionary Creator, pay extra attention to these reflection prompts. Use them any time you're feeling the need to break free, to break things before you break down, to define solutions, when you're into analytical mode and overanalysing and over engineering everything, when you crave ease and effortlessness. Use them when you're craving space and freedom. Use them to nurture your liberation fuelled heart that believes every soul deserves to know what it is to be free of whatever real and perceived limits, blocks, restrictions and patterns hold them back. If you don't yet know your Archetypes or are unsure if you are a Visionary Creator you can 100% benefit from these reflections. We each have parts of all 12 Thrive Factor Archetypes within us, so a month of Visionary Creator inspired reflections will certainly be exciting and freeing for you.

- **What actions should I take to clearly see what needs to be done in order to achieve the outcome I am working towards?**
- **What kind of creative expression do I love the most and how can I do more of it?**
- **What sort of creativity is effortless for me so I can create every day?**
- **How can I celebrate my achievements and acknowledge my accomplishments?**
- **In what situations do I trust the gifts of vision and clarity that are innate in me?**
- **What does it mean to me to be creative?**

- When I 'see' what is possible for someone else or their business, how can I share that vision so it is embraced and not ignored?
- What obvious clues exist in other people's responses that are important for me to pay attention to? How can I recognise when I have 'gone too far' and need to build a bridge between what I see (and know) is possible and what others can connect with in the current moment?
- How do I define femininity and how can I see the strength that being female offers me?
- What am I willing to do to connect with and express my feminine side?
- What armour or shields do I put in the way of expressing who I am?
- How can I release my armour and allow myself to be vulnerable?
- What am I fearful of and how can I release that fear?
- How can I accept that everyone has a valid opinion and allow myself to value what others have to contribute?
- How can I trust the clear visions I get as valuable and know they can be trusted and followed?
- What role does creativity have in my life and business?
- How can I increase the amount of creativity and creative expression in my life and business?
- Who can I rely on to remind me to take regular breaks from work to have fun, be playful and in my life?
- What thoughts and behaviours are red flags for me; signs that I am too 'in my head' and need to get back to daily creating and self-care?

afformations

The Visionary Creator's afformations are designed to expand self expression, opening you to trust your intuition and to guide you to express the inspiration you are for all who have the honour of being in your life – personally and professionally. Working with afformations creates expansion and a dynamic that opens you to experiencing even more celebration. When you ask the right questions and get playful with discovering answers for them, anything is possible. Afformations are fabulous for journaling, visualisation or meditation prompts or simply for reflecting.

- What if I trusted what I see?
- What if my knowing was guiding me towards the most incredible outcome?
- What if my creative expression was my superpower?
- What if the way I supported others to transcend their limits was valued more than I realise?
- What if my ability to sense into the future and know what is possible, is a reality I can rely on?
- What if my vision could become a reality?
- What if the way I strategically approach things created ease and creativity for myself and others?
- What if my inner artist was a part of me I nurtured each and every day?
- You could create more afformations of your own to embrace the Visionary Creator themes.

creative exercise

Daily Mandala with the themes of Self Expression, Self Trust and Self Wisdom

With creativity so important to the essence of the Visionary Creator, this is the month to play with colour and connect with the parts of you who desire to be expressed in the world without words.

A mandala has its origins in eastern culture and in its simplest form is a circular expression of colour, shape and design. Mandala art is ancient, dating back more than 2,000 years. It is found in many cultures and used in many different religious and spiritual practices worldwide. I first came to love creating them when I understood aspects of their history and diversity for self expression whilst completing the first year of my Advanced Diploma in Transpersonal Art Therapy in 2005. Mandalas are said to symbolically represent life and its constant cycles and interconnection.

The Mandala is a round form that holds a story – our story - about our mental, emotional and spiritual state of being. Mandalas create a safe place to pursue feelings and explore complex patterns of our identity enabling us to gain insights and understanding to support us to expand self trust and celebrate the innate wisdom within. Each shape, colour, form and pattern is significant for the experience of creating a mandala. That said, creating one is most beneficial when it is done without too much thinking and analysis involved. Creating with freedom of expression and trusting your choice of colour and the lines you are intuitively drawn to create is the magic of a mandala creation.

It has been said that mandalas are symbolic pictures of the human psyche as it reaches out towards wholeness. For this month they are the way to connect with the gifts of the Visionary Creator Archetype by tapping into her innate self expression and love of colour and design as a way to bring life and insight to her visions. Creating is her soul's language.

The word mandala comes from the ancient text of Sanskrit and is derived of the root words 'man+da' which means essence. A man+tra is an essence captured within a sound. To Manda is added the suffix la, which means container or vessel. Therefore, the connotation of mandala is that it is an essence held within a container, in this case a circle with no beginning and no end. A safe space within which to create and express.

While you can learn a lot about mandalas with a quick search online and easily download printables of mandalas to colour, avoid doing that. Certainly, look online or in books for inspiration but don't let the intricacies of some mandala creations daunt you. Your mandalas are going to be most powerful to you if they are simple and feel effortless and fun to create.

They can shift your mood, provide insights and understanding and become an expression of that which you wish to experience in your day or week. You choose when you want to create your mandala and aim to create them daily if you can for the entire month.

your creative exercise invitation

For this month you are going to connect with your inner artist. But know that there is absolutely no artistic skill required.

What you need:

- A sense of adventure
- Unlined paper in your journal or a notebook, or even loose leaf paper
- Coloured pens or pencils
- Something circular to trace around like a large glass or coffee cup, or even a saucer if you like more space.

For as many days as you desire this month, your invitation is to create a daily mandala to connect to your innate self expression.

Follow these simple steps to create your Visionary Creator inspired mandalas.

What to do:

1. Take a new sheet of paper and create the outline of a circle wherever it feels best to place it on the page
2. Have your coloured pens or pencils ready to use
3. Set an intention by asking a question or using an afformation as a focus for the mandala. For example you could ask "let me see what is most useful for me today/right now?"
4. Start in the centre of the circle and fill the space with whatever colour, pattern, shape and design flows from you

5. Once the circle is completely filled (you can leave white space if this is part of the design!) look over what you have created
6. Reflect on any insights, messages or themes your mandala has for you
7. Write these either in your journal, or around the outside of your mandala in a way that feels expressive for you
8. Be sure to date the page and you may wish to capture any intention or question you asked too!
9. Over time, reflect on any changes you see in your mandalas, day to day, and record any insights in your journal or notebook to honour your creative expression and what it has to offer you this month
10. Consider how you have expanded your self expression, self trust and self wisdom throughout the month and celebrate all you have experienced.

Thrive Tip: At any time you desire more clarity of vision, create a colour filled mandala and journal on your creation. You never know what this creative grounding practice could bring you.

VISIONARY CREATOR
SELF-CELEBRATION CHART

this month I...

Played with colour	★★★★☆
Tried an artistic pursuit I have always wanted to try	★★☆☆☆
Added more meditation or visualisation into my days	★★★☆☆
Trusted what I knew and could see	★☆☆☆☆
Journaled to define my bold vision for the future	★★★☆☆
Shared my vision with others	★☆☆☆☆
Created personal mandalas to honour my self expression	★★★☆☆
Visited a gallery or place that inspired my creativity	★★★★☆
Allowed myself to see that I am creative in my own way	★★☆☆☆
Expressed myself in my style with what I wore all month	★★☆☆☆

Sign up for a year of Bragaudacious self celebration at www.thethrivefactor.com/bragaudacious

self-celebration from around the world

"Celebration was something that once a upon a time was rare and only saved for very big things (which had high value to others more than me) the down side to this was I was forgetting the little simple things that brought joy and sparked a glorious light within me, to acknowledge the tiniest of moves that evolved me and moved towards my goals I realised was where I needed to move my energy because this allowed more awesomeness to show up. This led to addressing some beliefs and mindset challenges that were holding me back from celebrating.

Now celebration is a beautiful magical part of my day as well as my week and monthly check ins, gratitude is the most simplest form of celebration for me a thank you may be simple but it delights and expands my soul sometimes the thank you turns into a happy dance as the joy flows from me. This growth now also sees me settings rewards to celebrate different achievements big and small these celebrations could include a wide range of things like a simple ritual bath, coffee out by myself or with someone else, buying a plant, a day of rest and self care in the form of a home spa day, going for a trip to the beach, celebrating with a new book or my favourite at the top of the list is new art supplies.

There is one other type of celebration I would like to mention and this is birthdays these weren't always happy times for me a few years back I reclaimed this day it was the day my soul choose to start this glorious and chaotic life journey so I felt I needed to find an aligned way to reclaim this for myself which includes about 80% of the day for just me no expectations from others just me giving to myself and my soul whatever it needs in that moment and then family get me in the late afternoon evenings - I love to meditation, spend time in a bath or by the ocean and order in some divine organic chocolate to eat while journaling"

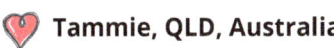 **Tammie, QLD, Australia**

"I celebrate my wins by ordering takeaway! Bigger wins, I'll get champagne, too ;) As for traditions, one of my yearly favourites is going to the apple orchard with my family to pick apples every September and then to the pumpkin patch in October, where we all pick our own pumpkin!"

 Cassie Howard, Toronto, Canada

"My favourite affirmation is "The more me I am, the wealthier I become." Which, of course, can be "The more me I am, the more I thrive""

 Jane McKay, Bruthen, East Gippsland, Victoria, Australia

"My celebrations can be very quiet, just that internal satisfaction of knowing "Yes, I did it!", but not averse to a nice bath, a good meal out, an excellent bottle of red or a walk somewhere special"

 Thrive Factor Coach, Caroline Smith, Perth, WA, Australia

bragaudacious sister, this is just the beginning!

Activate Thriving and Amplify Celebration

Who am I?
What am I here to do?
What's my purpose?
How can I make things easier?
How can I create a meaningful life?
A positive impact business/career?

A series of questions deeply connected within the collective unconscious of every person on the planet. Well maybe not the business one but exchange business for whatever word resonates. As a smart, ambitious woman you want to know who you are and what kind of impact you're here to make. It's part of your innate design and human curiosity to want to know.

Tapping into the treasure of archetypal psychology takes you directly to the source of the answers you've been seeking. No more wondering or questioning or imagining. No more judging or misunderstanding. The Thrive Factor framework and her 12 unique and gorgeous Archetypes were created for women in business and leadership. Knowing your Thrive Factor fast tracks your connection to who you are and taps you into your effortless success zone. #truth

It's foundations of ancient wisdom, refined with hundreds of women over the last decade plus gives you trust knowing what you learn about yourself is your truth. There's so much to celebrate when you know who you are. Acceptance, compassion, energy, motivation, drive, creativity, and a true sense of happiness and more is waiting for you.

When you activate thriving, amplified celebration becomes inevitable.

Embrace and be a Leader in the Sisterhood of Self Celebration

Women have been coming together since the dawn of time to be in circle, to learn, to share and to celebrate. We can be masterful at celebrating each other but find uneasiness in celebrating ourselves. By choosing to open to the journey of self celebration, Bragaudacious style, you become a role model for other women.

Every self celebration infused action you take tells your sisters around the world that celebration is for her too. You are leading by example and being a part of the collective voice in support of self celebration.

Invite your friends, peers, colleagues, your sisters in life, work and business to join you on this quest. Be inspired by the great shift available for us all when we collectively rise together and actively self celebrate. The monthly themes you have enjoyed in Bragaudacious are awesome focuses for women's circles, book clubs and more. Anytime you gather with your sisters use it as a chance to begin a conversation about celebration and guide each other to talk openly about self celebration.
The more we all do this the more we open to thriving in joy filled ways.

Bragaudacious on the Socials

I love spending time on social media and right now my favourite platforms are Instagram and Telegram and you can also find me active on Facebook. I get such a buzz out of seeing you share anything related to my work or content and you being inspired makes my entire year. Please reach out and follow me on my active social channels. If you search Shannon Dunn or Thrive Factor it should be easy to find me. Tell me you're joining the thriving woman revolution thanks to one or more of my books or a podcast interview or some other way you have connected with me and then please freely share your inspired moments with an abundance of self celebration vibe.

When sharing on social media here are some hashtags to use to make it easy for Team Thrive Factor to find you and connect!

#bragaudacious
#bragaudaciousmoments
#proudtobragaboutme
#celebratingthriving
#thrivingwomenrevolution
#thrivefactor
#thrivefactorarchetypes

Thrive Factor Coaching

I am so proud and excited to bring this book to the world three years to the month since my international award winning The Thrive Factor book became a reality. In that book I mentioned a future opportunity to undertake a certification to become a Thrive Factor Profiler. I am delighted to confirm that became a reality in the middle of 2019 and now, as we begin 2022 the certification has evolved and is now extended way beyond my original bold Visionary Creator dream and is a Thrive Factor Coach™ Certification.

To share my work and ways of working with women worldwide to activate thriving has been a long held dream. To move through the evolution to expand into a new level wasn't necessarily comfortable but it was necessary.

You can read more about becoming a Thrive Factor Coach™ in the final section of this book.

the thrive factor coaches and celebration

"Growing up in my family, things were never really celebrated in a big way. No big deal was ever made, especially when it came to personal achievements. There was a quite 'well done', and then we moved on with life.

For much of my life, I had not taken the time to stop and celebrate my achievements and birthdays. Low self-esteem contributed to this – who was I to do that? I was not special? I grew up believing I would be "showing off" if I took the time to acknowledge and celebrate something I had achieved – that would be egotistical (and the Liberator Engineer aspect of me, who does not like ego, has been fully supported that stance).

Yet I loved so much to celebrate and cheer on others' achievements and successes – thank you Inspirer Believer. What I learned from understanding my Inspirer Believer is that she needs to celebrate and be inspired by herself – it is her greatest gift. She would find her effortless flow and thrive with so much more if she allowed herself to do so. OMG massive aha – I had permission to celebrate me and that I was not being egotistical in doing so.

I love to celebrate now.

Birthdays are super special as that is the one day that is about celebrating my life. I love to celebrate with family and friends with good food and a glass of wine. I love to celebrate when I receive a beautiful review from a client or sell out a course and have a successful week in business. I share it and feel proud of it.

I love to look back and celebrate all the obstacles and challenges I have overcome in my life, knowing that I achieved that because I chose to do the work. Yay – way to go Kim!

Sometimes I cheer out loud.
Sometimes I dance around the house.

Sometimes I share and celebrate with friends (especially other Inspirer Believers that I know love to celebrate with me).

Sometimes it's a night out.

Sometimes I treat myself to a day spa session or I buy myself something I have wanted for a while. And sometimes I find a quiet place to journal, reflect, smile, and be filled with gratitude and appreciation.

 Kim Herman, *Holistic Transformation Therapist,* **Thrive Factor Coach at** *kimherman.com*

"Celebrating my achievements and who I am as a woman has not been an easy journey for me. I grew up in an era where comments such as "too big for your boots" "full of yourself" "stuck up" and "too cocky" were the norm. As a child and teenager, I decided on a subconscious level that I wouldn't be loved or accepted if I appeared to be too excited about myself or what I was doing.

In discovering that I have the Inspirer Believer Archetype, I can see now how that subliminal messaging stifled my innate instinct to be excited about and share EVERYTHING. As a wiser and older version of myself, I now celebrate my achievements great and small, with a group of loving and supportive sisters I have in my life who celebrate with me.

I love to schedule in regular self care practices to celebrate and honour my personal and business growth, these include regular massages/facials, coffee dates with friends, Pilates and walks on the beach. My Advocate Rescuer adores this regular dose of self care and in ensuring that her needs are met, I avoid her tendency to want to help and fix everyone around her.

I also make a point of celebrating the information, knowledge, and life lessons that I have gained along my path and how much value these have added to my life and the work that I do. When witnessing positive change, transformation, and growth in the wonderful women that I coach, mentor, guide and support I honour the inner wisdom of my Mentor Teacher.

Celebration for my Shapeshifter Alchemist Archetype, of course, has many forms and can change often. Keeping track of all that I have manifested, created, earned, and achieved, through tracking sheets, mandalas and gratitude journaling are fun and creative ways that I celebrate as a Shapeshifter

Alchemist. Understanding the strengths and challenges of my four Thrive Factor Archetypes has given me greater clarity into ways in which I can celebrate all that I am and all that I do, these support me in shining and thriving"

 Kerryn Slater, *Inspired Spiritual Alchemist, Self Discovery Coach,*
Thrive Factor Coach at holisticessentials.com.au

"With a strong Mediator Diplomat, celebrations are always likely to be low key. It's just enough to know it was a job well done, no need to make a fuss about it. And besides, she's a perfectionist, so when other people might be celebrating, Mediator Diplomat might be asking "how did I get that wrong?"

Not that she can't celebrate. I remember working in an organisation where the agents would frequently put the phone down, punch the air and announce, "I'm going to write up an offer". I was working as their bookkeeper and payroll officer, so when I punched the air and said "Yes!", everyone stopped and stared and asked "What?". "Super balanced first time", I replied, thereby convincing all that I was quite mad. But to me it meant that I had finally found all the weird errors left behind by my predecessor, and for a perfectionist Mediator Diplomat, that is a real cause for celebration!

My Visionary Creator can also be low-key. She is well aware she sees things well in advance of others, so there is no point shouting it from the rooftops, as no one else will understand. So, she quietly recognises that the strategies are working and that encourages her to keep going, while others are saying "You must be regretting taking on this job". Six months later, they finally recognise the change.

When it comes to the artistically creative side of the Visionary Creator, celebrations can be a bit more flamboyant. Her strategies are always great, but selling an artwork is a wonderful but unexpected pleasure. The inner Queen is released, and champagne is demanded!

 Caroline Smith, *Profit Strategist, Certified Profit First Professional,*
Thrive Factor Coach at jackadder.com.au

meet shannon

A compulsive creator, visionary thinker, liberation loving, inspiration seeking, wisdom woman, marketing nerd, chai devotee, potentialist, disco tragic, and stand-up paddleboard enthusiast, Shannon Dunn is an international award winning businesswoman, business coach, retreat leader, and regularly sought out as a keynote speaker and presenter.

In February 2020 Shannon was opening keynote speaker at a week long women's event in Fiji, The Ultimate Girls Week Away alongside Eat, Pray, Love author Elizabeth Gilbert, a definite career highlight. Also motivation to get back to speaking and presenting internationally when this becomes a reality once again.

Founder of Thrive Factor Co (formerly Creative Possibility), Shannon is author of The Thrive Factor; Unlock Your Effortless Success Zone, a book enthusiastically introducing you to her archetypal framework that has been activating profound personal permission and changing the way women interact with themselves and the world by harnessing their mindset, marketing, money, and magnetism innate strengths, since 2010. As a long-time business coach driven to successfully coach women to expanding effortless success, Shannon helps ambitious women leverage their Thrive Factor, activate thriving, embrace their inner quiet rebel and turn their wisdom (all they know and have experienced) into profit without unhealthy hustle and overwhelm.

Shannon has been changing the landscape for women in business and leadership for over 25 years and is as inspired today as she was on day one of her business journey. Referred to by her loving, global client community as Biz Yoda, Shannon is a coach, teacher, and cheerleader to smart women who are coaches, creatives, and impact makers; Ingenious business women. What is an Ingenious woman?

She's unapologetically wants to be a success, invest in help, is determined and takes action to fast track bringing her future success into the present, understands the powerful dynamic of energy, thrives beautifully when she has support but also knows she's got what it takes to progress on her own – she simply desires to accelerate her success, integrates self awareness into her business/career, knowing how it amplifies everything and loves being a part of a sisterhood of other impact makers.

Shannon has a unique gift for meeting people where they are at, seeing and igniting their potential, holding space for radical transformation and liberation, and creating programs and solutions that lead to genuine, sustained thriving in life and business. In 2019 Shannon expanded the thriving woman revolution with the opening of Thrive Factor School. Through certification programs, she teaches women in business the art of Archetype Profiling and Coaching using the Thrive Factor Framework™ so they can take their clients and business to an entirely new dimension of thriving, starting with the highly valued experience of self awareness and celebration.

Drawing on the gifts of her own four Thrive Factor Archetypes and infused with a commitment to lead by example and practice what she teaches, Shannon has a bold vision to certify at least 440 women who are Licensed Thrive Factor Coaches by the end of 2030. In doing so she is growing a community of connected, wise, caring, inspirational women championing thriving for themselves and other women globally as Thrive Factor Coaches. Find out more about Shannon, following her on the socials, her coaching and consulting work and retreats and working with her by visiting
www.thrivefactorco.com/shannon-dunn-links

Shannon's four Thrive Factor Archetypes provide insight into the creative, freedom loving, cheerleading, inspiration seeking, wise woman she is. This is how Shannon describes her four Archetypes.

Inspirer Believer is aka my excitable cheerleader! She's full of inspiration and loves to share what excites her. Often that's you so please keep showing up and sharing who you are and what you do. She gets totally into the things that make sense to her and help her to understand her place in the world and reason for being here. These belief systems guide her expression in the world. As the potentialist she has an effortless ability to recognise the greatness in others and adores seeing you rise to meet and expand beyond your possibility. She's a muse for the world, super creative and crafty and her greatest lesson is to allow herself to be inspired by who she is and what she's putting into the world. Everything got better when I did this!

Liberator Engineer is aka the bossy, rebellious one! She's a big picture woman who can see all the moving parts and fine details. The world and everything in it is a puzzle she adores solving to create freedom for one and all. She acts fast, building and engineering systems, frameworks, models and solutions like no one's business. Each has a sole purpose - to bring liberation and true freedom to herself and others. She's cool and calm on the outside but has intense emotions and if she's not feeling free you better watch out because she can implode or explode. Volcanic style! I love her energy, quick wit, super capable intellect, strategic view and her rebellious nature.

Mentor Teacher is aka as the endless learner and compulsive sharer! My inner wisdom woman. She sees and absorbs the lessons in everything. Books, courses, life. She has a gift for sharing knowledge and wisdom in a way that helps others accelerate their learning and embodiment of lived and learned experiences. She is off the charts wise but can forget that sometimes. She's a huge part of my business and why one of the many words I use to describe myself is educator. I can't help but share what I know with the intention that everyone benefits from the wisdom I have and knowledge I gather. When I teach, I am totally in my effortless success zone and adore teaching a diverse repertoire of topics relating to thriving, the Thrive Factor Archetypes and the 4 M's of Momentum: mindset, marketing, money and magnetism.

Visionary Creator is aka the strategic one and the big bold dreamer! One of the rarer Archetypes I've seen in the 1000+ profiles I've completed, she's a divine blend of vision and strategy, creativity, and magic. Intellectual and dreamy she needs to create (mostly in artistic ways) to ground her visions so they can more effortlessly become reality. Her foresight and futuristic sense are admired and valued by all who experience them. She has a gift for collaboratively guiding others to connect to different time and spaces, often in an imagined future realm, to connect with resources which are embodied and become available in an amplified fashion in the present. If you want to understand this dynamic, learn about the magic and vision of shamans the world over. She's wise like the Mentor Teacher and when she learns to trust what she sees she's a force to be reckoned with. I love her boldness and foresight and use her all the time to challenge myself and my clients to dream and do bigger, brighter, and bolder. She's the key to my thriving and could be the key to yours!

become a thrive factor coach™

In the middle of 2019, some nearly 6 months after the publication of The Thrive Factor; Unlock your Effortless Success Zone, the next piece of my vision to ripple thriving out into the world by activating thriving in as many women as possible became a reality.

This was when the first group of students joined me in the initial certification program offered by Thrive Factor School, the training aspect of my company. As a premier training provider with the International Institute of Complimentary Therapies (IICT), Thrive Factor School initially offered a Certification in Thrive Factor Profiling. Just two years later this certification was relaunched and is now a Certification in Thrive Factor Coaching, in recognition of the expansion of this body of work and the value of working with a Licensed, Certified Thrive Factor Coach™.

If you're a coach, consultant, mentor, counsellor, or therapist working with women then the Certification in Thrive Factor Coaching could be the game changer you and your clients have been looking for!

I find many coaches and women working with a female centric audience use some kind of foundational system, methodology or framework if they truly create sustained evolution in the work they do with their clients. I get asked a lot about why I use the Thrive Factor Framework™ as the foundational, first step in all my coaching experiences with clients. Aside from the fact I created it - yes it is an original work - I use it because it's a thorough, proven, expansive opportunity for women to take self awareness and self understanding to the level of true embodiment.

Sure other things can create this. But I find when you're leveraging psychology on a personal level with individuals you shift beyond the bright-shiny-focus-on-$$-not-outcomes coaching and mentoring and your clients experience a personal revolution from the inside out. One that lasts. It impacts every area of their life and career/business. Positively impacts. They continue to expand into the success they desire. It's not just present when they work with me or while they're paying me.

Self awareness may seem like a soft skill you don't need to focus on. That's a huge misconception. Self awareness, the centre of the Thrive Factor Framework™ and all she stands for, leads to expanded personal leadership, emotional intelligence, irreversible mindset shifts, money EQ, ease and effortlessness, focus, self celebration and infinitely more depending on what you desire and what your Thrive Factor Archetypes actually are!

Becoming a Thrive Factor Coach™ places you in a exceptional advantage at this pivotal time when the community is small and expanding. You have a genuine opportunity to establish yourself as a coach who uses a proven psychological framework designed to activate thriving through profound self awareness and self celebration. So cool!

Become a member of the Thrive Factor Coach™ community by enrolling
in the Thrive Factor Coaching certification. Information about the student guide, certification details and enrolment can be found at **www.thrivefactorco.com/shannon-dunn-links** or reach out to team Thrive Factor at **hello@thethrivefactor.com** for more information.

www.ingramcontent.com/pod-product-compliance
Lightning Source LLC
Chambersburg PA
CBHW061819290426
44110CB00027B/2922